Taming the Wild Tube

Taming the
WILD TUBE
A Family's Guide to
Television and Video

by Robert L. Schrag

The University of North Carolina Press
Chapel Hill • London

©1990 The University of North Carolina Press
All rights reserved
Manufactured in the United States of America
Library of Congress Cataloging-in-Publication Data

Schrag, Robert L.
    Taming the wild tube : a family's guide to television
and video / by Robert L. Schrag
        p.   cm.
    Includes index.
    ISBN 0-8078-1892-5 (alk. paper).—ISBN 0-8078-4272-9
(pbk.: alk. paper)
    1. Television and children—United States.   2. Television
programs for children—United States.   I. Title.   89-35663
HQ784. T4S346 1990   CIP
791.45′083—dc20
The paper in this book meets the guidelines for permanence
and durability of the Committee on Production Guidelines for
Book Longevity of the Council on Library Resources.

Manufactured in the United States of America

94   93   92   91   90   5   4   3   2   1

To Susan, Andrea, and Emily

Contents

Acknowledgments

"Acknowledgments" is one of those words I remember learning how to spell—like Mississippi. When I first saw it written, I was sure my teacher was playing a joke on us. No real word had that many letters and began with "ACK." After accepting that it was a real word and learning its definition, I remember thinking, "That sure is a complicated way to say thanks." Later I came to realize that just saying thanks isn't always enough. This is one of those times, hence the following acknowledgments.

The perspective of this book is a direct result of lessons I learned in my own family. My father, a sociologist by trade and training, always insisted that we consider what impact our own lives were having upon the society of which we were a part. Around the dinner table most kids have to report what they did that day. "How was school?" "Did you get a hit in the ball game?" "How was rehearsal?" We too had to make that report; but most days, and in many ways, we were also asked to answer the question, "What are the sociological implications of your life?" The question stuck.

My mother, through her actions both within and outside our home, has always made it clear that children are the world's most powerful and precious resource. It is from her that I learned that the most honorable work one can do is the nurturing of children, for in children is the preservation of the world.

It is only natural that this book's attitude reflects the combination of those two parental perspectives.

However, no body of work is solely the product of good intentions and proper perspective. One must also have both professional opportunity and professional support. Hence, I need to thank David Perry, my editor, whose initial encouragement and continual guidance cleared many thickets from my path, kept my spirits high, and made the whole project possible. I also need to thank William Franklin and William Jordan, past and present heads of the Department of Speech-Communication at North Carolina State University, who not only tolerated but actively supported and encouraged my often nontraditional research endeavors.

I also need to thank the many students in my criticism classes who served as sounding boards and guinea pigs for many of the practices and premises set forth in this book.

Finally, I need to acknowledge the three women who run my home and to whom this work is dedicated. My wife, Susan, read the first, second, and third drafts of the manuscript and was never shy about pointing out the weak spots. My older daughter, Andrea, drew my attention to the central concern in the work more powerfully than any body of coursework or literature could hope to do. Watching her grow up with television was invaluable to the theory-building aspects of this exploration. My younger daughter, Emily, came along just in time to test the practices that evolved from those theories. She has already suggested some revisions and extensions for a second edition! I trust that you, the readers and users of this book, will do the same.

Introduction
Confessions of a Bookworm in a TV World

A few years ago I was poking around in the attic of my parents' house when I came across an old blue blanket. The blanket itself was not being stored—it had been used to wrap up something of greater value. I forget what that object of greater value was, a picture or a vase I think. But I will never forget that blue blanket—the one with the scorch mark up toward the corner. It was, of course, my blanket. And the scorch mark has a story.

I have always loved to read; it remains what I consider my most self-indulgent form of entertainment. However, the scorched blue blanket is evidence that reading is not always the safe and sedentary form of amusement we usually perceive it to be. When I was a boy my parents' late-night plea was not, "Turn off the TV and go to bed!" Instead they would call up the stairs, "Turn out your light now, put your book away, and go to sleep."

My response, "I'm almost done with this chapter," was a far more flexible plea than today's "The show's almost over." The latter only works at five minutes before or twenty-five minutes after the hour. At any other time the parent knows it is a ruse.

One night I had milked the "I'm-almost-done-with-this-chapter" gambit beyond the limit. My mother had come up to the room and turned off my reading light herself, leaving me in darkness. There was a pitiful little moon that night so I could not resort to heavy squinting by moonlight reading—a practice that has rewarded me with wonder-fully thick glasses. But there was still enough light for me to make out the shape of my book lying there on the nightstand.

I do not remember what the book was, but I do remember that I was only a few short chapters from the end, and that I *had* to know what happened. Sleep would be a vain pursuit until I had followed the plot through its final turning. So I resorted to another of my standard ploys. I took the shade off my lamp and pulled the light and my book down under the covers with me. In my newly constructed tent I plunged back into the now forbidden pages of my book. I read furiously until the heat of the light bulb drove me out to gulp cool breaths at the open window. I panted for a while, staring out into the night, and then slid beneath the covers and back into the world of my book.

I had never fallen asleep in my reading cave before, but I must have been exceptionally tired that night, because I started awake to the smell of scorching fabric and opened my eyes to see the first small curlings of smoke rising from the blanket, now resting in direct contact with the light bulb.

I flung back the covers; cold night air rushed in and shadows jumped about the room as I replaced the lamp on the nightstand. I quickly turned the light off and sat there in the dark listening to the pounding of my heart.

"Never again," I vowed to myself. "Never again." And it was a promise I kept—for almost a week.

A little bit of that remembered fear crept back as I sat there in the attic, running my fingers over that old piece of scorched blue blanket. But what came back much more strongly was the memory of all the nights I had journeyed off through countless worlds and across the centuries with the books I had secreted away in my forbidden reading cave.

Many people find it paradoxical that an incurable bookworm makes his living teaching about, reading about, writing about, talking about, and watching television. But it is really not that strange. Reading could take me anywhere and bring me safely back again, and it still does the same for my children. We have read to our girls almost every night of their lives. Neither the seven-year-old nor the two-year-old will willingly go to sleep without her nightly book. Withholding reading time is our most severe form of punishment.

But books have a powerful competitor for my children's attention. Television, too, is a dreamweaver, every bit as enchanting as the printed page—and in some ways more so. We—as parents, or care-givers, or teachers—must come to grips with this medium. Television will *not* go away and most families will *not* choose to do without it. Those who suggest otherwise engage in wishful thinking. Furthermore, the demise of television would, I contend, create far more serious problems than it would solve.

But our relationship to television, particularly as it affects our children and our families, can no longer be a passive relationship. It is true that television spins technicolor fantasies for our children and brings them more information than most of us were ever privy to at their tender age. But we need to examine the quality of those fantasies and assess the values that lie behind them; we need to consider the range and impact of the information that television draws into our home. We must domesticate this medium and make sure that it does not chase its print-bound ancestors from our rooms or, most importantly, from the rooms of our children.

This, then, is a book about television. It is neither a book of praise nor a book of condemnation. It is a book, as the title says, about taming television. It is in some ways a story, a story about how families can live happily and productively with a controlled television set. And I will tell you the story the only way I know how—from one bookworm to another.

Taming the Wild Tube

I

Television and You

I had occasion to visit one of those new video "superstores" the other day. I thought for a moment that I had stumbled into the control room of the Starship Enterprise. Three large walls of television sets blinked in unison, a salesperson was demonstrating a new "camcorder" about the size of my old 35-mm camera, while another customer fiddled around with Sony's pocket-sized "Watchman" color TV—amazing clarity on a 2½-inch screen. I crouched beneath the satellite dish for a moment, overcome by the science-fiction aura of it all. But then I remembered that even though contemporary video *seems* like something out of *2001*, in reality it is uniquely an artifact of twentieth-century America. As a communication medium, video is international in scope, but it has drawn much of its form and content from American commercial television. Video is the one thing that truly unifies our diverse country—the one thing we all have in common.

If some cultural anthropologists from the planet Whatzit were to visit the United States, they would be confronted with a richly textured, complex culture. Language choices shift from English to Spanish, from Spanish to Polish, Polish to French, French to Yiddish, back to English again—and then you leave New York City. Foods range from crepes to collards, from enchiladas to étouffé, from sushi to sizzle-lean; but we all are bound together by the staples of pizza and peanut butter, burgers and fries. Our citizens come in every size and shape, every color and creed, reflecting every occupation and avocation under the sun. We are truly a potpourri of humanity.

Yet, as different as we appear to be, we share that unifying characteristic that I mentioned just a moment ago. In most every hogan and hotel, in tepee and trailer, behind frame walls or stucco, in mansion and hovel alike, in the bedroom, the classroom, in cars, boats—and now even walking down the street—there flickers the glow of America's televisions.

Like it or not, the one element of our society that we all have in common is our television. We watch it . . . we watch it a lot. Consider these numbers:

1. Between 1984 and 1986, Americans bought 42,909,000 new television sets. We spent over $12¼ billion on those television sets.
2. Ninety-eight percent of all American homes have television sets. Most of those are color sets, and many homes have more than one set.
3. There were almost 1,300 television stations operating in the United States at the end of 1986.
4. There are 7,800 cable systems in the United States, serving almost half of the nation's television households. Most of those systems offer at least 20 channels, and some offer 60 or more.
5. Advertisers spent almost $20 billion on television commercials in 1985.
6. The television in the average American home is on for more than seven hours a day.
—*1987 Broadcasting and Cablecasting Yearbook*

So it is obvious that we watch a lot of TV. But were our observers from Whatzit to conclude that we were all engaged in the same occupation they would be making the same mistake that we often make as parents. They would have failed to realize that television is no longer "something" we do; it is a wide variety of "somethings" we *can* do. Television, with the diversifying impact of cable, has finally begun to approximate that great video bookstore that media proponents have always dreamed about. But, the problem is that our video bookstore, like every bookstore I have ever been in, has a problem with quality control. In bookstores there are racks full of literary classics, romance novels, westerns, cookbooks, pop psychology books, diet and fitness books, even books about television, and at least several magazines about every topic under the sun. However, of the thousands of titles available in the store, all but twelve will either waste your time or bore

Reprinted with special permission of King Features Syndicate, Inc.

you to death. OK, I exaggerate, but you get the idea. And I'm sure I will hear few objections when I say that the ratio of good material to bad is even worse on television. But that is precisely why we need to be so very careful about how we shop in our video bookstore—careful about how we consume TV.

This book is an attempt to help us become better consumers, more cautious shoppers, if you will, when we venture into the video bookstore. This chapter starts us on the way by examining who owns the bookstore, and what it is selling.

Who Owns the Bookstore

If you spend, as I do, a good deal of time talking to "videotypes" you will inevitably hear someone assert, "TV is an art form wrapped up in a business." I really wish that were true—at least then there would be an art form in there somewhere. The real picture, I am afraid, is that television is a business wrapped up in a business. We might even want to amend that statement, in light of the advertising revenues listed above, and say, "Television is a big business, wrapped up in an even bigger business."

There was a time when you could say that NBC, CBS, and ABC owned the bookstore, but not anymore. I am not arguing that those three networks no longer dominate television, but there are cracks in the old foundations. ABC was recently bought out by Capital Cities and it is now Capital Cities/ABC Inc. Ted Turner is only one among several who have launched attempts to buy CBS. I have not heard that anyone is trying to buy NBC, but that is probably because they are afraid they might have to bid against Bill Cosby, whose show remains the cornerstone of that network's profits. The venerable networks, once the sole owners of the bookstore, have therefore become market commodities themselves. And satellites and cable systems have brought a whole new cast of characters into the ranks of owners of the bookstore: superstations, news networks, sports networks, and arts and entertainment channels have all rushed into the newly expanded—and potentially lucrative—video bookstore.

The point is that television networks, stations, and production companies are all businesses, and like most businesses they have one overriding objective—to make a profit and pay a dividend to their stockholders. So the bottom line is this: business executives, responsible to their stockholders, own the bookstore—and their only job is to maximize profits.

Finally, we need to realize that not many people own the bookstore. While programming choices may well be expanding, it is by no means an open shop accessible to every writer, director, or producer with a good idea. Rather, as with newspapers, the actual number of individuals and corporations that control contemporary television is getting proportionally smaller, not larger.

How the Bookstore Makes a Profit

For the most part television makes a profit by selling commercial time. (We will, for the time being, exempt PBS from this discussion of profit and the selling of commercial time. But it seems to me that those sponsor logos are getting larger and larger all the time.) The programs themselves generate no income per se. They are merely vehicles for the commercials that *do* generate income for the bookstore owners, lots of income, more than $20 billion a year of income.

That seems like a lot of money to "buy time." But the advertisers are not buying time, they are buying people. They are buying you and me. Actually they are buying a network's ability to deliver you and me to their commercials. The advertisers are betting that the network can get us to sit down in front of the set at a specific time to watch their commercials. They firmly believe that we will, after watching their commercials, be more inclined to go out and purchase their products, thus generating income for their companies so they can pay a dividend to their stockholders and so on and so on.

Answering the natural question of *why* advertisers are willing to bet $20 billion a year on this process brings us to a consideration of the Great American Ratings Game.

The Ratings Game—or Pat, I Want to Buy an Audience

We have all heard of the "ratings." Whenever our favorite program vanishes from the airwaves, or is placed "on hiatus," we understand that it "was having trouble in the ratings." In plain English that means that not enough people watched the program to make it an attractive commercial vehicle for advertisers. It's as simple as that: the ratings book comes out and Linda Ellerbee is out of work again. But how do "they" (the ratings makers, Nielsen, Arbitron, etc.) *know* how many people are watching that program? Have they ever asked you? Probably not, and it does not really matter because they ask enough other people to make some very accurate guesses. Here is how it works.

The ratings report the viewing choices of a sample audience that has been carefully constructed so that it duplicates, as closely as possible and on a much smaller scale, the national television audience. The ratings people then are able to gather fairly reliable information about national viewing behavior by getting very detailed information from this relatively small group of people—usually 1,500 to 2,000 families in a national television ratings sample (Nielsen uses 1,700).

These families usually fill out a viewing diary. In the diary they are supposed to write down when the set is on, what program they are tuned to, and who is watching. Since the ratings makers are legitimately concerned about the accuracy of this self-report form of audience measurement, the data are often backed up by electronic monitoring of the TV set. This monitoring can range from a relatively simple indication of whether the set is off or on and tuned to a particular channel, to the quite sophisticated data provided by the people-meter.

The question most commonly asked about ratings is, How can they know from that small group of people what the whole country is watching? That takes us back to how the sample is put together. Although it is called a "random sample," that is a misleading name for it, because it implies that the ratings company just wanders out into the streets and randomly gathers up the first 1,700 people they come across. But such a sample would be anything but "random" in a scientific sense.

Say you want to gather a sample group of thirty people to tell you what they watched on television last night. If you ask where you can find thirty people quickly, a logical answer in contemporary America is "the Mall." So you head off to the local shopping mall and buttonhole thirty people at the Chocolate Chip Cookie Emporium. And there you have your random sample. Right? Wrong. You have systematically excluded certain segments of the population from your survey.

First, you have excluded from your sample everyone who does not shop at that mall. That includes non-mall shoppers and people who shop at other malls. Second, you have excluded from your sample everyone who works at the time you took your survey, since being at work prevented them from being chosen for your survey. Third, you have excluded everyone who does not buy chocolate chip cookies at the Emporium. That includes people who are on diets, people who prefer homemade cookies, people who are allergic to chocolate, and those strange people who just do not like chocolate chip cookies.

The point of a "random sample," in a statistical sense, is to create a sample in which every single person in the country has an equal chance of being chosen. The Nielsen company draws their sample from U.S. census maps using *multistage area probability sampling*. This method allows them to draw a national sample that gives them enough accuracy to satisfy their clients—the television and advertising industries—at a price those clients are willing to pay. It allows them to make a very good guess at what most people are watching at any given time. While the data gathered from these sampling techniques are getting more and more sophisticated, they are still aimed at defining as precisely as possible three basic numbers: HUT, Share, and Rating.

Homes Using Television, or HUT

HUT is one of the three basic bits of information that ratings makers use to compute their magic numbers. It means exactly what it says—Homes Using Television—but it is given as a percentage of all the available homes.

For example, I live in Raleigh, North Carolina, which is in Wake County. Wake County has, according to the *1987 Broadcasting and Cablecasting Yearbook*, 136,100 television households. But rarely, if ever, are all those households using their televisions at the same time. So the ratings people compute percentages. Let's say that 87,456 of the television households have their sets on at a particular time. To compute HUT we take those 87,456 households and divide them by the total number of television households, 136,100. That gives us 64.2 percent or a HUT number of 64.2. Now, that HUT number not only tells us that 64.2 percent of the television households have their sets turned on, it also tells us that the measurement was taken during prime time, because it is a fairly high HUT number. Obviously, if advertisers want to reach a lot of people with their message, HUT is an important number for them.

Share of Audience

Share is the percentage of homes tuned to any given channel. Let's say that the numbers above came from Monday, February 23, 1987, at 8:00 P.M. The major network choices in my market at that time were a "Bob Hope Special" on NBC, "Kate and Allie" on ABC, "MacGyver" on CBS, and "Planet Earth" on PBS. Let's pretend that 25,321 sets were tuned to "Kate and Allie," 22,872 to "MacGyver," 21,642 to "Planet Earth," and 17,621 to "Bob Hope." We would compute each station's "share" of the audience by dividing its number of sets by the total number of sets in use.

"Kate and Allie"	25,321/87,456 = 28.9%	or a 28.9 share
"MacGyver"	22,872/87,456 = 26.1%	or a 26.1 share
"Planet Earth"	21,642/87,456 = 24.7%	or a 24.7 share
"Bob Hope"	17,621/87,456 = 20.1%	or a 20.1 share

(Because decimals are rounded, percentages, shares, ratings, etc., may not total exactly 100.)

Early 1988 brought a significant change to the ratings game. Spearheaded mainly by Roger D. Percy, the "people-meter" is a high-tech interactive ratings meter that requires audience members to punch in a control number before they begin to watch the TV. Arthur Unger examined its impact on the television industry on April 20, 1988:

People-Meter Shock at the Networks

People-meters are causing upheaval and controversy in the television business. The reasons:

—People-meter figures show a decline of about 10 percent in prime-time audiences. This translates, according to some network researchers, into a loss of $50 million in advertising revenues.

—People-meter figures have reported great variations in evening news audiences. NBC's Tom Brokaw was No. 1 until the people-meter figures placed Dan Rather in the No. 1 spot, soon to be superseded by ABC's Peter Jennings, who has now been replaced by Dan Rather again. Mr. Brokaw, meantime, has been No. 3 for several weeks in a row. NBC tends to blame it all on the people-meters.

—People-meter figures indicate that there has been as much as a 20 percent decline in viewing of Saturday morning children's programs.

Will People Push the Buttons?

Network researchers, hardly unbiased observers, claim the confusing and contradictory data are often misinterpreted by those who make the greatest use of people-meter demographics—advertising agencies. Methodology is a major bone of contention. Will people punch themselves in faithfully? How should the fact that some will not do so be taken into account in the calculations?

Bill Rubens, vice-president of research at NBC, says he is troubled by the button-pushing aspect. He is concerned that not only children but adults will try to avoid punching themselves in and out. "Maybe what we need is implantation," he joked recently. "But then diary keeping was a problem, too."

David Poltrack, vice-president of research at the CBS Broadcast Group, says, "Half the people asked to participate [in the people-meter surveys] don't participate.... There is a technology-related bias—high-tech people comfortable with television and video technology are much more likely to participate. And, obviously, their viewing patterns are different from the general population's."

Allen Banks, executive vice-president and media director of Saatchi & Saatchi DFS Compton, part of the world's largest advertising conglomerate, probably reflects the advertising community's attitude toward the new technology when he says, "People meters represent a great advance in television research, even though they are still in an evolutionary stage."

Shares allow broadcasters and advertisers to assess how well stations in any given market are performing against their local competitors.

Rating

Finally, the magic ratings. A rating reflects the percentage of all possible television households that are tuned to a program. So the ratings for the programs in our example would be computed by dividing the sets tuned to each program by the total number of televisions in the market.

"Kate and Allie"	25,321/136,100 = 18.6%	or a rating of 18.6
"MacGyver"	22,872/136,100 = 16.8%	or a rating of 16.8
"Planet Earth"	21,642/136,100 = 15.9%	or a rating of 15.9
"Bob Hope"	17,621/136,100 = 12.9%	or a rating of 12.9

The three basic numbers of the television ratings game can be summarized as follows:

HUT—The percentage of homes with the set turned on at any specific time.

Share—The percentage of homes with sets turned on that are tuned to a given station at a given time.

Rating—The percentage of all television households, not just those with the set turned on, that are tuned to a given station at a given time.

But what do those numbers mean? How are they really used? Broadcasters and advertisers use them in several ways, but what most affects you and me as viewers is the way in which they are used to compute a "cost per thousand" figure for an advertiser. (Those in the industry call this CPM, which would seem to mean "cost per million" until we remember that "M" is the Roman numeral for thousand. Somehow it seems strange to me that high-tech wizards use Roman numerals, but then the world of television *is* strange.) The amount of money that a broadcaster can charge an advertiser is directly dependent upon the number of viewers the broadcaster can promise will be watching the program that surrounds the advertiser's commercial. That in turn allows the advertiser to compute a comparative cost per thousand.

Let's say an advertiser was going to spend $1,500 for a local thirty-second commercial for Sam's Tire Center. To look at the difference in cost per thousand let us compare the highest-rated program, "Kate and Allie," with the lowest, "Bob Hope." On the station showing "Kate and Allie," Sam would pay $1,500 to advertise his tires to 25,321 households. By dividing 1,500 by 25.3 we discover that Sam would pay $59.28 for every thousand households—that is his "cost per thousand" on "Kate and Allie." Now, on the station showing "Bob Hope," Sam would pay the same $1,500 to advertise his tires to only 17,621 households. By dividing 1,500 by 17.6 we discover that Sam's "cost per thousand" on the "Bob Hope" station would be $85.23. It does not take inside information from Wall Street to figure out where Sam is going to get the better deal.

In reality, Sam would not have to pay the same $1,500 at the lower-rated station, because that station would not be able to charge the same rate as the higher-rated station. The station showing "Kate and Allie" could actually charge Sam $2,000 for the thirty-second spot, and it would still be a better deal than $1,500 at the station carrying "Bob Hope"! Why? Because Sam's cost per thousand households at $2,000 with "Kate and Allie" is $79.05 instead of the $85.23 per thousand it would cost him if he paid the $1,500 to the "Bob Hope" station. So to meet the cost per thousand rate on the station showing "Kate and Allie," the "Bob Hope" station could only charge $1,390 for that thirty-second spot.

The differences become even greater when we apply them to a national commercial. Let's assume that our ratings are national, not local ratings, and let's interpret them on the basis of the 86,104,900 national television households. Since each ratings point equals 1 percent of the available households, we know that 16,015,511 households are watching "Kate and Allie" (based on their 18.6 rating). We also know that the 12.9 rating for "Bob Hope" represents 11,107,532 households. Let's assume that Sam's business, now the National Tire Company, is going to spend $150,000 for a national thirty-second spot. The cost per thousand households is $9.37 for "Kate and Allie" and $13.50 for "Bob Hope."

Again, the reality is that networks do not charge the same amount for commercial time. The network with the more highly rated program can charge more per minute—often significantly more—and still

Reprinted with special permission of King Features Syndicate, Inc.

be a better deal for advertisers in the actual cost of reaching large numbers of consumers.

The bottom line on all this numbers talk is that the most highly rated programs in the most popular time slots generate the most profit for their networks; and that each network's goal is to make as much profit as possible. As consumers of this industry's programs we need to be aware of how these financial realities affect the programs we watch.

What Gets on the Shelves

The commercial structure of our television industry is such that the people who run the bookstore do not care at all about the quality of the product on the shelves. I do not mean that they do not care in a personal sense. I am sure that a number of executives at ABC were genuinely sorry that they "had" to cancel "Our World," with Ray Gandolf and Linda Ellerbee. It was, after all, one of the finest representatives of electronic journalism we have seen in the last decade. An excellent teaching tool that drew insightful and understandable meaning out of our nation's past, "Our World" was a joy to watch. But it did run opposite "Cosby," and, while profitable, its numbers were not good enough to make it all that profitable. *That* is what I mean by "do not care." For the industry, the measure of what is good and what is bad is quite simply "what is popular? what is profitable?" It is getting a little more complex as refinements in audience research are allowing the industry and the ever-present advertisers to ask, "What is popular among those individuals with a significant amount of expendable income?" But that is just a variation on the same basic theme.

There is good news and bad news in this twenty-first-century, strangely run, video bookstore. The good news is that it keeps television free from significant political bias. The recurring charge that various networks demonstrate some type of political bias or another loses whatever bite it may have had when we realize that television networks are terrified of offending anybody. The simple reason for that fear is that if they offend someone, that particular someone may not watch their programs, and the ratings would drop. Then the network would not be able to charge the maximum rate for their commercials, profits would fall off, and important people would begin losing their jobs.

The bad news is, of course, that we tend to get very bland television, aimed at some demographically "average" American who probably does not even exist. Some folks argue, and quite persuasively, that this blandness, this social sameness is itself a kind of cultural bias. One may wish to debate that, but at the very least the middle-of-the-road posture of most television encourages conformity and discourages uniqueness.

Furthermore, normal television fare has indicated time and time again that there is precious little room for artistic concerns in an industry that aims for mass popular appeal. As a common bit of folk wisdom says, "Nobody ever went broke under-estimating the taste of the American public." This claim is borne out by the actions of Ted Turner, who is using new computer technology to "colorize" classic old black and white movies that came under his control when he bought MGM's film library. Never mind that there is something cheap and degrading about *Casablanca* in garish color, never mind that the director designed the shots as black and white visual compositions, the ratings indicate that colorized movies drew larger audiences than black and white ones. So Turner—who, by the way, is now one of the owners of the new video bookstore—continues to colorize them, saying, "I bought them, they're my movies. I can do whatever I want with them."

But perhaps the worst news is that we have only ourselves to blame for what we get on commercial television. Commercial stations give us exactly what we tell them we want. All those data about audiences do not *only* tell advertisers what shows to buy time on; they also tell producers what kinds of programs we like to watch—and the producers proceed to give us more clones than a mad scientist ever dreamed of.

And Now the Shelf Marked Cable

Cable television is a relatively new part of the store. Its beginnings can be traced back to the 1950s when this new medium—commercial television—was moving out of the big cities and into the countryside. There it ran into mountains and valleys that, while undeniably picturesque, got in the way of broadcast television signals. Someone then got the idea of putting a big antenna up on top of the hill outside of town—where reception was good—and running wires from it back to all the sets in town. Thus was CATV (Community Antenna Television) born. And so it stayed for a few years. But television, like nature, abhors a vacuum. I mean once you had all the networks piped into town you still had seven or eight channels just sitting there on the set, not doing anything. So the cable entrepreneurs began to do things with them. I remember a particularly fascinating channel on the first cable system I subscribed to—an automated camera simply panned back and forth endlessly across a thermometer, a barometer, and a clock. It was not a terribly popular channel until the night someone snuck in and pinned some rather racy photos over the weather gauges. (This could be where Hugh Hefner got the idea for his Playboy Channel.)

But from those humble beginnings today's multibillion-dollar cable television industry grew. Cable is quite different from the broadcast shelf of the bookstore because most cable companies derive less than 5 percent of their gross revenues from advertising. Cable companies have to pay more attention to meeting the programming requests of their subscribers since they are paid, in part, directly by those subscribers. The other way that cable companies generate revenue is by attracting customers to "premium channels" like HBO, Showtime, or the Disney Channel. These programming services then pay the cable company a fixed rate per subscriber. The point is that advertising becomes a secondary concern, and programming becomes more important. This results in a more diverse set of program offerings as cable operators strive to bring a blend of video offerings that will tempt the jaded palate of today's TV viewers. From porn to prayer it's all out there in the wonderful world of cable.

Shopping in the Bookstore

There are a number of things we need to keep in mind if we are to be effective consumers in this great American Video Bookstore.

1. *The bookstore has good things to offer.* Our tendency is to be discouraged by the overwhelming amount of pre-packaged mediocrity that

Reprinted by permission of UFS, Inc.

we see arrayed around us everywhere. We need to keep in mind that there are excellent things available if we only look carefully.

2. *The bookstore isn't designed to make it easy to find good things.* The bookstore is designed to make money, either by selling our attention

to advertisers or by selling packages of programs through cable systems.

3. *The bookstore doesn't care about you.* So you need to take care of yourself and your family by making wise choices about how to shop in and use the bookstore. The next few chapters in the book are designed to help you do precisely that.

4. *The bookstore can be changed.* To assume that "television is" something specific and unchanging is as foolish as the assumption that we are all doing the same thing when we "watch television." The industry can be changed as our interactions with it change. It is an industry that is quite sensitive to shifts in the public's preferences, since its very existence depends upon its ability to please that unpredictable audience. Chapter 6 is designed to help you begin to change the industry in ways that are beneficial to you and your family.

As we begin to assess and restructure our relationship with the glowing presence in the living room, remember that TV itself is neither good nor bad. It is a simple electronic device that is capable of bringing messages into our homes. We can use it foolishly or wisely. My intent is to help you use it wisely.

2

Into the Minds of Babes

Mark Twain often said, "I came in with Halley's Comet, and I have every intention of going out with it!" My coming in did not coincide with the arrival of a comet, but my birth was synchronized with the ascent of a star, for I "came in" with Uncle Milty and the "Texaco Star Theatre!" However, I harbor no delusions about going out with that star, since I realize that Uncle Milty will somewhere, on tape, cable, or video cassette, be making people laugh long after I "go out." But our simultaneous arrival in the fall of 1948 does make me one of the earliest "TV Babies." Technically there were some earlier TV Babies, made possible by an hour or so of "regularly scheduled evening programming" on ABC, NBC, CBS, and DuMont scattered throughout the early 1940s. But the fall of 1948 was, by far, the most ambitious television season in the new medium's history. I came in not only with the "Texaco Star Theatre" and its host Milton Berle, but with "Arthur Godfrey's Talent Scouts," "Meet the Press," and "Kraft Television Theatre"—all honored names in the history of the tube. (I must also admit to sharing my initial fall season with "Kobbs Korner," "The Adventures of Okey Doky," and "Captain Billy's Mississippi Music Hall," all of which are better forgotten.)

Even though I was born into a world sporting four networks offering several hours of programming per night, my claim to TV Babyhood is highly suspect. The medium was there all right, but by today's standards, neither the programming nor the audience was. There were barely a hundred stations scattered throughout the country, mostly in major cities. TV sets were large pieces of furniture that could fill the ends of living rooms but sported screens hardly bigger than a bread box. The medium was still just a rich man's toy that drew crowds to department store windows. And the most accurate answer to the dominant question of the last half of this century—"What's on TV?"—was, for eighteen to twenty hours a day, literally "Nothing."

My daughters—Andrea and Emily—have, for better or worse, no trouble laying claim to the label of TV Babies. Andrea could work a VCR with her feet by the time she was two. She could walk and had fingers, but she had discovered that if she pushed the buttons with her toes she didn't have to leave her "fully-prone kid's preferred viewing position" to fast-forward, rewind, or pause the tape she was watching. Emily is still a touch young for such feats, but I have no doubt that her big sister will teach her the requisite skills once she discovers that a little sister sometimes works better than remote control. Still, Emily may have the purest claim to being a TV Baby since I first saw her on television, as a tiny head and backbone on a sonogram machine. Now, when sleep escapes her in the wee hours of the morning, we often lie on the couch together watching things like "The Story of the Fur Seal," while I explain to her variously serious, smiling, and crying eyes the intricacies of the Arctic food chain being played out before us.

What should we proto-TV Babies do with our children, the real TV Babies? Is there anything we can do to control the effect of this medium that takes up so much of their time? I know, I know—"Toss the thing out!" That response makes us feel good when we say it, but in reality it is a lot like spanking—it purges the emotions, but does more harm than good in the long run. It smacks of the parents whose firm stand against nudity in any form deprives their children of the experience of seeing the works of Michelangelo, Rodin, and Henry Moore. There is a better answer, and that is to teach our babies about television. If you start telling your baby, as I did with Emily when she was six weeks old, about the ins and outs of television, then it is not unreasonable for you to expect that baby to grow into a toddler and a child with good solid television habits. Emily's big sister did it, so can she, and so can your children.

Tiny Little TV Babies and the Myth of the Media Barrier

From the moment of birth an infant is able to take in and process information. He has a set of powerful mechanisms that allow him to control his universe, that allow him to respond with true discrimination to the sights and sounds around him.
—Dr. T. Berry Brazelton, "Neonatal Behavioral Assessment Scale" (Spasticks International Medical Publications, 1984)

My wife, Susan, and I have been through two pregnancies in the 1980s. The pregnancy that resulted in Andrea occurred while we were in our early thirties, while Emily claimed the pregnancy that began the latter third of our "thirtysomethings."

Anyone having a baby today (particularly that growing group of "folks our age") learns a number of dos and don'ts for a contemporary pregnancy. *Do* eat protein and vegetables, drink milk, exercise, rest. *Don't* drink alcohol, smoke, medicate, or vegetate. A lot of this behavior came from the new health kick of the last ten or fifteen years, but a goodly amount of it came from the painful lessons we learned in debunking the myth of the placental barrier. Our parents were taught that there was some magic barrier in the placenta that kept harmful things in the mother's blood from reaching the fetus.

The thalidomide-induced birth defects of the fifties and sixties began to give us disconcerting evidence of the fragility of that barrier. In the seventies we witnessed the tragedy of the addicted babies of drug addicts and the ravages of fetal alcohol syndrome in the babies of heavy drinkers. The past few years have tragically shown us that the AIDS virus also has no respect for the placental barrier. We now know that the placental barrier is much more porous than our mothers had been led to believe, and we act accordingly.

Given the pain and suffering it took for us to gain this precious information about the placenta, I continue to be amazed at our persistent belief in the myth of the media barrier. We seem to think that infants are protected by some electronic barrier from programs that others around them are watching. On numerous occasions I have witnessed babies parked in strollers, cribs, and playpens in front of "General Hospital," "The Young and The Restless," or some other afternoon dose of stress, arguments, and infidelity. The prime-time equivalent is babies getting their evening feeding or playtime in front of "Miami Vice" or "The Equalizer." In either time slot, babies soak up a couple of hours worth of conversations and situations which, *in the real world*, most parents would find unsuitable. But because they are *television* situations, we expect the media barrier to shield our babies from any possible negative effects of these programs.

"Now wait a minute, Robert," I hear you saying, "are you trying to tell me that infants understand what is going on during a soap opera or a shoot 'em up? And that these programs are somehow going to warp their little minds?"

My answer is no and yes. No, the baby is not going to understand what is going on in the program. But yes, the repeated viewing experience may well have an undesirable effect. Let me hook a couple of explanations together. I remember listening to Pete Seeger talking about a lullaby he was about to sing on a radio program. The lullaby was in Spanish, so he offered a brief translation, but then ended by saying something to the effect of "You don't really need to know the words, it says what all lullabies say—'Shut-up, go to sleep.' " And he was right; I did not understand the words, but the mood of the song was calming, gentle, restful—in any language. All babies speak lullaby: they may not do what you want them to, but they understand the mood and the overall intent, "Shut up, go to sleep."

Experience and experiments tell us that the inverse is true as well, that babies feel, and share in, our stress and anxiety. Our older daughter could have starred in a Steven King novel as "The Baby Who Never Slept." She was not an unhappy baby, she just never slept. Those of you who have had such a baby realize that they can introduce a significant amount of stress into your life, causing you (every once in a while) to actually exchange cross words with your spouse. So, when Andrea would drift into the light slumber that passed for sleep, Susan and I would attempt to fit a day's necessary conversation into some hurried whispers before losing consciousness. We could usually get away with that unless we began to exchange some of those cross words mentioned above, at which point Andrea would wake up and begin to cry. I am firmly convinced that it was the *tone* of the conversation that disturbed and awoke her. Sound familiar? My heart goes out to you.

But I wager that even those of you who do not have a high-strung baby have experienced your infant's ability to tune into and react to your stress and anxiety. Let us consider, if you will, the "crazy hour." The crazy hour (which can actually last several hours) is that time when the primary wage earner returns home from his or her workplace and attempts to interface with the primary caretaker who is attempting to prepare the major shared meal of the day—in my house it happened when Dad came home from work while Mom was getting dinner. But, however you shift the roles and time slots around, the "crazy hour" emerges when conflicting times and schedules, differing concerns and priorities, all meet around hunger. If your baby does not drop into instant colic during this time period, begin to make arrangements right now for his or her elevation to sainthood. Most babies tune into the crazy hour like a satellite dish, amplify it, and send it wailing out again like a fine stereo receiver.

The point is that babies seem to pick up on the emotional tones of the environment that surrounds them. Television programs are tightly edited, scripted, and scored to create a specific emotional impact. The television industry pours years of experience and millions of dollars into making sure that scenes of conflict and drama carry the maximum amount of emotional sights, sounds, and "punch." If you are going to sit down and watch some television with your infant, make sure that it will result in the emotional climate you want for you and your baby. Remember, there is no media barrier, and your baby is the most sensitive receiver you are ever likely to carry around.

I am often asked which programs are good for infants to watch and listen to, and which ones are bad. I tend to hesitate a good deal when confronted by that question, since the tone of every household is unique, as every baby is unique. Emily can listen to loud symphonies and raucous sports programs that would have sent her older sister into a frenzy at the same age. But let me provide some general suggestions for you that can be refined for your own household and viewing habits.

Bad Shows for Babies

Soap Operas

To be perfectly honest, I cannot think of any audience that should watch these programs, but they seem particularly problematic for infants because the tone of the conversations is almost always worried, angry, upset—all those elements that contribute to the crazy hour. But, rather than depict the occasional flare-ups of real life, soap operas present to their viewers—adults and babies alike—a never-ending stream of confrontations. If normal household stress can create a crazy hour, just imagine what subjecting an infant to the concentrated stress of soap operas can produce.

Prime-time Serial Dramas

These nighttime relatives of daytime soaps raise many of the same concerns about conversational tone. Furthermore, they add the element of visual violence. Visual violence is less of a problem for infants than for toddlers, because infants are not aware that the bright orange image is a car exploding with people inside. But there is still a legitimate concern regarding facial expression. We have all sparked a smile from our baby with our own smile, and conversely we may have also inadvertently induced a whimper as we frowned at a stubborn diaper pin or tape. We get these reactions because babies love faces and are amazingly adept at translating the expressions of those faces at very sophisticated levels.

How sophisticated? Well, psychologist Judith H. Langlois of the University of Texas at Austin reports a study that indicates a level of interpretation that goes well beyond the recognition of Mommy, Daddy, happiness, sadness that we have come to accept. In several related experiments Langlois and her colleagues showed to babies from two to eight months of age color slides of women that several hundred college students had rated as either moderately attractive or moderately unattractive. The investigators observed how long the babies looked at each slide in the attractive/unattractive pairs presented to the babies, and discovered a clear preference for the attractive woman (*Science News*, May 16, 1987, p. 310).

Although the faces on the *Dallas*-type programs are attractive enough to capture a baby's attention, unfortunately they are also often stressed, angry, somber, tearful, but attractive faces. Furthermore, the voices on these programs are often confrontational, arguing voices, and we should not be surprised if our infants respond to them by crying.

Prime-time Action and Adventure Shows

Oddly enough, these programs are probably less of a concern, visually, than the prime-time serial dramas discussed above. How can that be when these programs tend to contain more violence than the serial dramas? True, the action dramas "Miami Vice" and "The Equalizer" are far more violent than the serials "Dallas" and "Dynasty" (unless we include the season-ending episodes of the serials wherein several major characters must either die violently or be placed in imminent danger of so dying). But the violence in the action programs is of a kind far outside the realm of an infant's experience—far outside most adults' experiences as well, thank goodness. When babies see bombs blowing up, machine guns firing into speeding cars, the seemingly ever-present fuel dump exploding, etc., etc., the events have no meaning for them. The violence only becomes violent when one has learned what bombs and guns and explosions do to people. So babies could probably watch endless chase scenes and be harmlessly amused by the quickly shifting patterns of lights and colors. But that observation does not make it all right for infants to watch these programs. Some other elements get in the way.

Close-ups. Again, the human face is an important element. In most cases, gun fights, car chases, and other standard bits of TV mayhem are intercut with close-up shots of the faces of the participants. Most often, these faces are totally expressionless, allowing us to draw the intended emotion—anger, fear, determination, or whatever—from the context. But occasionally emotion creeps over a character's face. Pain always seems to call for a mandatory close-up. Try grimacing in pain at your baby sometime, but only when you are ready to do some soothing afterward, because a painful grimace often sets off a sympathetic wail from the little one. This potential for unpleasant faces remains a primary problem in allowing your baby to "watch" "Miami Vice" with you.

Sound tracks. Sound actually concerns me more than faces, since faces are fairly easy to avoid by simply moving the baby away from the TV screen. But if you try to move the baby out of earshot, odds are you both have to leave the room. And there are many things about action program sound tracks that may trouble infants. We need to remember that the sound track is a very powerful portion of many programs. Let me give you a personal example.

I first remember fooling around with the power of sound tracks when I was directing a one-act play for a theater course while a sophomore in college. The play dealt with the young wife of a whaler who was accompanying her husband on a voyage when the ship became caught in the ice of an Arctic winter. A great deal of the action is motivated by the boredom, silence, and danger of that isolated environment. In order to duplicate that feeling for the audience I decided to attempt to replicate the ringing in the ears that you get when listening hard to nothing. A friend of mine, who was taking a course in physics that contained a unit on sound, managed to obtain a tone generator, which I adjusted to a barely audible hum—like some distant, gigantic, soprano mosquito—and left it on throughout the play. It drove the audience absolutely crazy. It was not a terribly sophisticated ploy, I realize, but effective nonetheless.

Television sound tracks are infinitely more effective than my heavy-handed efforts, and they carry a bigger emotional impact. The sound track of an action drama is designed to suck you into the adrenaline rush of the action—lots of sound effects, lots of suspenseful, tense music. These audio elements can, even if no one is watching the program or attending to the story, raise the stress level in the room significantly, and we have already talked about babies' unique ability to put ambient stress into crying patterns that will bring the strongest parents to their knees weeping. Hence, we need to be aware of the stress-inducing tone of the action drama sound track and its possible impact upon the baby who comes in contact with it.

There is another possible effect of particularly offensive sound tracks that we need to be aware of—the shutdown effect. In discussing his work with newborns, Dr. Brazelton observes, in *Infants and Mothers*, their ability literally to "shut down" their sense receptors. According to Dr. Brazelton, a newborn certainly is not at the mercy of his environment, but has a marvelous mechanism, a shutdown device, for dealing with disturbing stimuli: he can tune them out and go into a trancelike state. But Brazelton goes on to assert that this shutdown requires an amazing amount of energy, and babies will eventually be reduced to thrashing about and screaming. It seems clear, then, that if we park babies in front of very loud and very bright television programs, they may initially appear to go to sleep—when in reality they are avoiding a bad situation the only way they can, and we will hear a lot about it later.

So, as you can see, for infants who have no notion of content, there aren't really bad programs per se. Yet there are a number of elements that occur in many programs that may disturb your baby. Fortunately at this stage the cure is quite simple.

What to Do about Bad Shows for Babies

Get the TV set out of baby's line of sight. There is currently a good deal of debate going on as to how soon babies can see, how far away they can focus, whether they prefer complex patterns or more simple shapes, etc. But most experts agree on one thing: for babies it is still a case of "out of sight, out of mind." When very young infants are placed where they cannot see the television, they will—for a few brief blessed months—have no inclination to look for it. So turn them around and let them watch you instead of the television—at this point in their lives you are still their favorite program.

Turn the sound way down. You cannot use the TV to drown out the cries of a baby anyway; we've already seen how a loud TV simply makes a crying baby louder. So drop the volume to the point where you can follow what's happening, but still blunt the negative impact of the sound track. When you do this you will discover two things immediately. First, you will discover that, no matter what the broadcasters say, commercials are significantly louder than the programs. Second, you will discover that you are willing to trade most things you possess for a remote control with a mute button that allows you to turn the sound completely off during the aforementioned commercials and during long action sequences that are heavy on the noise and devoid of dialogue.

Good Shows for Babies

First of all, let me stress that there are no television programs in the world today that should be given preference over holding your baby, talking to your baby, playing with your baby, or even changing your baby. People are the ideal companions for babies, not television screens. Busy boxes, toys, mirrors, all these things are better for your baby than television because they stimulate movement, activity, and curiosity.

However, I realize that in our society babies and television are destined to coexist, and the advice "Just say no to TV" is not only arrogant but foolish. There will come a time when a harried parent will park the stroller in front of the TV because, in terms of the narrowed goals of peace and quiet, it works. While this is an impulse we do need to resist as often as possible, on the occasions when we do give in, let us remember to avoid the situations listed in the "Bad Shows for Babies" section and consider the following criteria.

As with "bad shows," our concern is not with content, since television stories are meaningless to a baby. Rather, we need to be concerned with the audio-visual elements of programs that a baby might find beneficial. Also, we want to begin our initial consumer training at this stage in the baby's life by associating positive experiences with programs we will want the baby to view later when content does become important. Keeping those concerns and objectives in mind, let us consider the following suggestions.

Stimulating Programs

Some babies do not relate to toys. Our older girl was a "people baby." She could care less about balls and rattles and blocks and rings—she wanted to look at faces and play with people. Hence, during those inevitable times when Andrea had to be left alone she was not very happy with those inanimate entertainers left in her crib or playpen. I do not recall exactly when it was that Andrea discovered "The Lawrence Welk Show." The program had long been a video staple in my wife's home, and she and I retained a genuine affection for the simple entertainment that it offered. So it was not unusual to find the program playing on our television, providing background music for the afternoon or evening household chores. One day we discovered Andrea, still less than two years old, rolling about, laughing and cooing—eyes riveted on "Lawrence Welk." From then on it became one of her favorite programs, and she would lie—toes literally "a-tappin' " with little baby dances, listening to music from another era. I strongly suspect that her early fascination with the show sprang from three elements, the faces, the movement, and the music. For her "Lawrence Welk" provided stimulation. There were lots of close-ups of big, smiling, happy faces accompanied by swirls of color in the dance numbers and pleasant melodies throughout. While "Lawrence Welk" is a hard program to find in many markets, we recently discovered that the Welk Music Group, headquartered in Los Angeles, has begun to market a number of videotapes of "The Lawrence Welk Show."

Viewing environment. If we are using television as a stimulating activity, then it is imperative that we give the baby room to roll around in, to wiggle in, to play in. This is not the time to wheel the stroller, or the baby recliner, up to the television set. Put down a blanket, or pull up the playpen, and be sure to stock it with those disdained toys just in case the baby does get motivated to play along with the program.

Big happy faces. As I mentioned before, when you laugh babies laugh with you, but they will not give you the luxury of crying alone—they will howl right along with you. I do not think people were allowed to frown on "Lawrence Welk," and our baby would grin right along with those big happy faces. Today we find a lot of big happy faces on— where else?—game shows. Those marvels of greed and consumerism do afford us with a wildly high percentage of ecstatic faces. Largely because they rarely, if ever, focus on the losers. The drawback on these programs is that the sound tracks are engineered by former rock musicians who sold out to the glitter of daytime TV. The game-show sound track is the second most frenetic sound track on television—the first belongs to any fifteen minutes of MTV. But remember, a baby does not understand the sound track anyhow, so turn it off and put your own sound track on the radio or record player and let the baby enjoy the big smiling faces.

Cooking programs also have smiling faces on them; people rarely seem sad when they are making good things to eat. Julia Child remains cherubic throughout her program, and there is a lot of chopping, stirring, and whisking to hold a baby's attention.

Pleasant sound tracks. A pleasant sound track is very important for baby TV, where words have no meaning, but tone speaks volumes. Contemporary television does not have many pleasant sound tracks. It is easier to find them in syndication, on cable, anywhere you find old television with musicals and variety shows. The Disney Channel reruns the old "Mickey Mouse Club Show," and the "Fun with Music Day" is usually quite nice baby TV.

The visually pleasing cooking shows mentioned above have the added benefit of a tolerable sound track. No anger, no stress, very few shrieks and howls; yet they include a lot of happy talk—"Doesn't that look lovely? See that pretty color? My, doesn't that smell delicious?"— and lots of pleased chuckles and exclamations, too. They maintain a nice energy level without becoming frantic.

Tranquil Programs

These programs are chosen with the "crazy hour" in mind. Dr. T. Berry Brazelton, whose excellent books *Infants and Mothers: Differences in Development* (New York: Dell Publishing Co., 1969) and *Toddlers and Parents: A Declaration of Independence* (New York: Dell Publishing Co., 1974) now snuggle up next to Dr. Spock on many parents' bookshelves, describes one normal onset of the crazy hour:

> Daniel's parents took him to see his grandparents for a day's visit. They were utterly charmed by his cheerful responsiveness and his activity. His grandfather played with him all day. Two-year-old Mark sat huddled in his mother's lap, watching all this with quiet envy. Mrs. Kay did her best to comfort Mark and make up to him, but Daniel was able to keep the center of the stage for hours on end. Daniel took one short nap in the afternoon, but maintained a constant level of activity and interaction the rest of the seven-hour visit, responding to the new audience and all the stimulation.
>
> On the way home, he began to fall apart and had to be held by his mother. He screamed through his supper, refused all of the solids, and drank only half his bottle.
>
> Anna Freud speaks of the "disintegration" of a baby's or child's ego that goes on at the end of a day. This is an example of it. (*Infants and Mothers*, 127)

The problem with this disintegration of the ego and the crazy hour that goes along with it is that it usually occurs when you are least free to deal with it, during preparations for dinner or in the middle of the last load of laundry. These are the times when tranquil TV can be a godsend. Here are the qualities we need to look for in tranquil TV.

Viewing environment. This *is* the time for the stroller, the baby recliner, or the more restrictive travel crib. The idea is to create an environment for slowing down, nodding off, going to sleep. Dropping the brightness control on the TV set to a softer level does not hurt either.

Big pleased faces. Close cousins to big happy faces, but not quite. Big happy faces break into laughs and wind baby up further. Big pleased faces reassure, comfort, quiet. Fred Rogers of "Mister Rogers' Neighborhood" has the best Big Pleased Face I have ever seen, and that alone would make his program an ideal tranquil TV program for a baby. The cooking shows with the volume lowered a good bit also fit into this category, as do many other "educational" programs. These programs are all characterized by rather pleasant looking people talking in calm tones about pleasant pastimes such as painting and gardening. These qualities, and the absence of heavily produced sound tracks, make this type of programming a good choice for the crazy hour.

Tranquil sound tracks. As mentioned above, the sound of tranquil TV is very important. We are looking for sound tracks "in lullaby." The gentle spoken sound tracks of educational television are one option; lyrical musical sound tracks are another. The important thing to keep in mind about babies and sound tracks is that the sound track need not be directly related to the images on the screen. You can mix the pictures from "Growing Beautiful Roses" on cable channel 43 with any tape, record, radio station, or disc you please. Just mute the television and turn on the stereo.

There is one possible exception to this mix and match of audio and video. With the recent boom in home video gear, some innovative parents may construct custom-made tapes for their babies—on the correct assumption that babies will find familiar faces more interesting than stranger's faces. However, studies have demonstrated that babies form very accurate associations between their parents' faces and voices. When experimenters had a mother look at her baby while a tape of a stranger's voice was played, the baby was not happy at all. So if you are going to create a home videotape for your baby keep the faces and voices firmly grounded in reality.

Babies' Consumer Education

The last area of concern for our tiny little TV watchers is the one that may be of greatest importance in the long run—helping them establish good viewing habits. I realize that your infants are not going to sit down and have a dialogue with you about the relative merits of "Mister Rogers' Neighborhood" and "The Muppet Babies," but that is not the point. They do not sit down and discuss the value of vitamins and the four basic food groups with us either, but we begin to introduce them to the notion—experientially—as soon as they start solid foods. We need to begin to introduce positive television viewing models to them as soon as possible as well. I suggest you do this by creating positive associations between current situations and the kind of viewing behavior you want to see them acquire as they grow older.

This is not a major developmental scheme, but rather a suggestion for something that might help your children control television viewing throughout childhood. It is based on the notion that "as the twig is bent the tree will incline." We start bending the twig toward positive associations with good programs.

Let's use "Sesame Street" as an example. It is a program that, for reasons we will discuss more fully later, has a lot of good things to offer children. Because I want to encourage my baby to prefer "Street" to other kinds of programs, I nudge her in this direction by spending some time playing with her close to the TV while her big sister is watching the program. As we play I smile and show her Big Bird while saying, "Look, there's Big Bird! Isn't he cute?" You get the idea, it's a lot like "Here come some yummy carrots!! Watch Daddy eat the carrots!" You may feel foolish doing it, but it begins your baby's first exposure to the idea that we comment about what is happening on that screen, we judge it, we control it.

This is also a good time to begin to demonstrate to your baby that televisions can be turned off. When "Sesame Street" is over we can carry the baby over to the television and say " 'Street' is all over for today, let's turn it off now." And "click" we turn it off, a magic motion which—like eating vegetables—is never too soon to start teaching.

And just as it is never too soon to start teaching our babies about television, it is never too late for us to learn this other important message: *You are your baby's favorite television show.* Yes indeedy, nothing brings a smile to a kidlet's face faster than Mommy's or Daddy's own smiling face. Television should only be used as an occasional "time-buying-device" when you absolutely need some space and time to yourself—which is something we all need. However, if you come to depend upon television to entertain your baby, your baby will come to depend upon it as well. That is a dependency we all want to avoid.

3

Teach Your Children Well

I wanted to call this chapter "View from the Peanut Gallery," but I knew I could never get that past my editor. "Not bad, Schrag," I could hear him saying. "I know what the Peanut Gallery was, you know what the Peanut Gallery was—but how many of today's parents will really remember what the Peanut Gallery was?"

"The Howdy Doody Show" did go on the air before I was born, but it ran for over fifteen years—some of you who, like me, are "thirty-something" parents, remember that the Peanut Gallery was the place where the "Howdy Doody Show's" studio audience of screaming kids was housed. And that is what this chapter is about—the audience made up of kids, sometimes screaming, sometimes not.

When you begin to talk about children and television you enter into a very touchy area. There are some very sincere people out there who really believe that television is a demonic device that ought to be stuffed into another new device—the trash compactor—and reduced to little squares of transistorized debris.

For example Marie Winn, in her book *The Plug-In Drug* (rev. ed. [New York: Penguin, 1985], xi), maintains that "to work for better [children's] programs . . . is not unlike dealing with alcoholism by striving to replace cheap whiskey with Chivas Regal." Neil Postman asserts that television requires and develops no skills and has the potential to put our minds to sleep (*The Disappearance of Childhood* [London: W. H. Allen, 1983], 73–80). And even Jim Trelease—whose superb work *The Read-Aloud Handbook* I will rave about later—felt compelled to include a chapter that lists seventeen terrible things television can do to children (chapter 7).

The concerns of all these authors remind me a great deal of the story my father tells about Grandmother Schrag and the escalator. My grandmother lived, and through my young eyes enjoyed, a life that

would leave many contemporary Americans looking for someone to sue. Grandma Schrag was born during the waning decades of the nineteenth century and raised in a home chock full of the values and beliefs of the 1880s. She spent most of her life farming and raising her seven sons and two daughters on the fertile but unforgiving plains of southeastern South Dakota. It was a far more demanding life than most of us live today. The machinery of today's modern farms was still just a gleam in a tinkerer's eye. Central heating was rumor from the city, and air conditioning came courtesy of either a hand-held fan or a stiff wind down from Canada.

But it was also a simple life. Boredom and anxiety were epidemics that future generations would have to confront. There was always something to do: planting or harvesting, caring for the stock, the buildings, the land, the fences, and the family. As for worry, that seemed to center on the weather, the crops coming in, and the live-stock staying healthy. And those were all items on the agenda of the Almighty, so why worry about something over which you had no influence?

So Grandmother Schrag had a pretty solid handle on the world around her—until 1945 when my father got his Ph.D. Since Dad was the first, though not the last, of Grandmother's boys to go out and get this high falutin' degree, and since Grandmother and Grandfather had always placed such strong emphasis on education, it seemed only right that they should take themselves off to the wicked city of Chi-cago and witness the conferring of the degree.

Naturally, my mother and father wanted to show my grandparents all the wonders of the big city. And the visit went along excellently until the visit to Marshall Fields department store. Apparently, the family had spent a half-hour or so roaming the aisles of the first floor, admiring the wonders of big-city shopping, when Mom and Dad decided it was time to see what the upper floors had to offer. So they led Grandmother and Grandfather over to the escalators to ride up to the second floor.

When Grandmother Schrag saw the escalator she stopped dead in her tracks. She had never seen the like of it in all her born days—moving stairs. Now, she was willing to give city folks considerable leeway with their trolley cars, and their traffic, and their buildings that went up much higher than the good Lord probably intended, but she drew the line at moving stairs. Stairs weren't supposed to move, it just wasn't natural. And no amount of pleading, teasing, or cajoling could entice her onto that contraption.

So Grandmother Schrag left Chicago, having seen her son receive his degree, but without having seen the second floor of Marshall Fields. And she also left with the firm conviction that the good people of Chicago were headed straight to Hell on the shiny stairs of the down escalator.

Many modern parents seem to feel the same way about television. And, I think, for many of the same reasons. My grandmother knew about stairs. She had lugged the wash up and down them; she had carried babies up and down them; she had climbed them laughing and climbed them crying, in the stifling heat of the summer and the bone-chilling cold of a South Dakota winter. She knew stairs, and she knew what they were supposed to do. But the escalator was something quite different; someone had taken the old solid familiarity of stairs and twisted them somehow, making them strange and alien, frightening and tinged with danger.

As contemporary parents, we follow much the same train of thought but substitute TV for stairs. We know about television. We grew up with it, we have watched it almost every day of our lives. We spent our childhood with "Spin and Marty" and "Mickey Mouse," with "The Waltons," "The Brady Bunch," "Happy Days," and "Days of Our Lives." But as we sit down and watch the television that our children will be growing up on, as we watch MTV and "Voltron," and sample "Inhumanoids" and "The Equalizer," we get the feeling that someone has taken the old familiarity of TV and twisted it somehow, making it strange and alien, frightening and tinged with danger.

It is this fear of the unfamiliar, this discomfort with technological change, that seems in part to have motivated the comments by Winn, Postman, and Trelease that I mentioned earlier. And that is not hard to understand, because when we look at television, as adults, it is a frightening landscape we see. Many an evening my wife and I have hit the couch after putting the kids to bed, ready for an hour of "make-the-world-go-away-TV." Instead we find, as we run up and down the buttons of the remote, a seemingly unending stream of the loud, the violent, and the vacuous—and those are only the commercials!

How Children "See" Television

The good news is that children do not see television that way. Children define and relate to television very differently than do adults. Just how differently has been reported in a delightful book called *The Lively Audience: A Study of Children around the TV Set* (Boston: Allen & Unwin, 1986), by Patricia Palmer. I say delightful not in the sense that you would want to curl up with it in front of the fireplace— it is, after all, an in-depth report on a very complex research project— but rather in the sense that it tells us some important things about children and TV that have been overlooked for far too long. The book is able to do so because—unlike most experimental studies about children and television—the author and her colleagues went into the children's homes and painstakingly observed how they watched TV on their own turf.

According to the Palmer study, "One thing is certain: the wide-eyed mute and impassive child viewer who is constructed in the minds of adults and is the target of many television programs is nothing like the children who have been described in this study"(90). Instead the study discovered a group of children who liked, but were not obsessed with, television. The researchers found that children incorporate both the technology and the programs of television in their everyday play. Palmer writes, for example, about a couple of young viewers who pretended that the TV was a drive-in movie. They would "drive" up to the front of the set to watch their favorite programs. She also describes the intricate games children play away from the set, which are based upon the programs TV offers. In short, the study describes, as the title says, a "lively" audience.

But perhaps even more important than the debunking of the "couch potato" myth is what the study tells us about how kids define television. For adults, television is a huge industrial and commercial octopus with tentacles slinking into every nook and cranny of public and private life—more powerful than a speeding escalator. According to Palmer's study, that is not the way children see it. They see "television" as something limited to "those [programs] they chose to watch and named as favourites"(114). And that bit of information is very important because it reassures us, as concerned parents, by reaffirming the idea that *television is controllable.*

But it is easy to forget that we can control television. It is easy to give in to the adult paranoia that leads to Winn's thrashing about with whiskey bottles, Postman's image of slumbering brain cells, and Trelease's seventeen deadly sins. As adults, we get overwhelmed by the immensity of the media-industrial complex, and the resultant feeling of powerlessness angers and paralyzes us. That issue is important—*but it is not the one we need to resolve in our living rooms.* The issue that demands our attention in the home is, "What is television *to my family,* and how do we—as a family—control it?"

After thinking about it, I realize that I have seen evidence of Palmer's conclusions in our house. Many times when I am sitting in the living room watching the news, or a talk show, or a sporting event that does not interest her, Andrea will complain, "Daddy, why do we always have to watch your TV?" I had always assumed that this was just her way of saying, Why do we always have to watch your *programs*? But Palmer's study shows that it may well mean more than that; it may well mean that my programs are not even TV to her. And that means all I have to worry about is controlling *her* TV. That is still a rather tall order; but it's a darn sight more manageable than taking on *all* the combined forces of television.

Controlling Children's Access to Television

I realize that the idea of "controlling" your child's TV viewing has a terribly repressive ring to it, out of place for the reformers of the sixties and seventies who now wish to send their own children into the nineties with the best of all possible breaks. But let's examine the issue and the options. The issue, obviously, is whether or not children's access to television needs to be controlled. The fact that I am writing this book and the fact that you are reading this book are fairly good evidence that we agree that, yes, that access should be controlled.

People give a number of reasons why access to television needs to be controlled, but all those reasons are really variations on the most obvious reason: we have programs on television today that are just not appropriate for children, but they can still be seen and "understood" by children. Joshua Meyrowitz's book about the effect of electronic media on social behavior, *No Sense of Place* (New York: Oxford University Press, 1985), contains a chapter called "The Blurring of Childhood and Adulthood." In this chapter Meyrowitz discusses how television eliminates many of the barriers that existed between the adult world and the world of children when print was the dominant form of mass communication.

No argument there, I mean how many six-year-old kids can read *Lady Chatterley's Lover*? And even if the most precocious six-year-olds in pre-TV days figured out the words, they would have had—in most instances—no experience that could give the words *real* meaning. They literally would not have been able to picture what was going on, so the words would have no meaning.

The case today is a very different one: any six-year-old can, if allowed, turn on the soap opera that bills itself as "Love in the Afternoon." There adult language will be spoken, adult behavior will be overt, and adult intentions clear—dropping the six-year-old into a rather sleazy depiction of the adult world of love, lust, deception, and power.

Calvin and Hobbes. © 1985 Universal Press Syndicate. Reprinted with permission. All rights reserved.

So the existence of inappropriate programs is one reason to control children's exposure to television. But deciding which programs are appropriate and which are not leads us again into that area of uncertainty that we addressed in Chapter 2. And again I need to say that I can't tell you which programs are inappropriate for your children and your family—but you certainly can! And the first step in making those decisions is learning what the major areas of caution are—what you need to watch out for.

The Big Brouhahas of Children's Television

Talking to people about their children and television is a lot like talking to people about their children and toilet training, or their children and drugs or sex—it is always "somebody else's kid's problem" that we start out discussing. But after a while we work through that to the point where we admit that it is not "somebody else's kid" who has a problem with TV. We may even get to the point where we admit it is not just our child's problem with TV and acknowledge that *we*, as parents, have a problem with the way TV fits or, more often, does not fit with the way we would like our household to think and operate. It is at this point that we often find ourselves thrashing about in one of the three big brouhahas of children's television: Now, I realize that "brouhaha" (pronounced brew' ha ha) is not a terribly precise word. And I must confess I have never run across it in the academic literature in the field of mass communication or media criticism. But it does seem to fit the case rather nicely, if you take it to mean—as Webster does, "a loud confused noise, as of many voices."

Three issues in family viewing seem to lie at the center of the "loud confused noise" of television's many voices. These three brouhahas are the issue of developmental concerns, the sex and violence issue, and the issue of commercials and overcommercialization. Each is an important issue, and one that every family must address as it goes about the process of deciding what television programs to include in its family definition of television.

However, before we discuss these issues, I need to point out that when infants become toddlers, and when toddlers become preschoolers and elementary-schoolers, their roles in family viewing decisions change. When kids are infants, they watch only what you decide they should watch. This happens for a number of reasons. First, their life is defined by those things to which you choose to expose them. An infant doesn't even know there *is* another channel, let alone what's on it. Second, they tend, in most cases, to be unable to reach or work the television or VCR. Third, and perhaps most important, they have yet to learn that most time-honored of human activities—arguing.

For most families, these conditions are like snowflakes in the early spring—states of tranquillity that crystallize for a bright moment before being swept away to join the melting streams of program awareness, remote control literacy, and general contentiousness. The toddler's preschool peers or older siblings introduce her to the wider realm of television, teach her to run the remote and the VCR, and then argue with her when she seeks to use those skills to control the family TV.

What all this means is that when you seek to control the TV consumption of your older children, you will probably not be dealing with a passive populace. However, while this means that you will want to discuss the situation with them, it does *not* mean that you must—or should—turn control of the TV over to the children. We will talk more about this later, in Chapter 8 ("You Make the Difference"), but now we need to return to our discussion of the issues in children's television.

The Developmental Issue

At what age do certain kinds of messages begin to have certain kinds of impacts? When does a child begin to recognize that a commercial is a commercial? At what point does a child begin to learn from violent television programs that force is a "legitimate" method of problem solving?

One way to find help in answering these questions is to turn to Jean Piaget (1896–1980), by most accounts the dominant force in developmental psychology. Piaget spent many years observing children—primarily his own three, Jacqueline, Lucienne, and Laurent. From these systematic observations he came to the conclusion that the tendency of children's minds to organize information interacts with the information provided by the world around them in a series of either four or six predictable periods. I say either four or six because Piaget's developmental breakdown looks like this:

1. Sensorimotor stage	0 to 2 years
2. Preoperational stage	2 to 7 years
a. Preconceptual	2 to 4 years
b. Intuitive	4 to 7 years
3. Concrete Operations	7 to 11 or 12 years
4. Formal Operations	11 or 12 to 14 or 15 years

The difficult aspect of Piaget, at least difficult for me, is to figure out what he means by each of those stages. Still, I will do my best to condense some of the descriptions I have read of Piaget's first two stages so as to give you a general idea of the kinds of ideas that structure the developmentalist's view of the world.

1. Sensorimotor Stage

In this stage, lasting from birth until about two years of age, the infant refines and practices basic sense perception and movement, advancing from sucking and startling to using a spoon and walking, from merely seeing and hearing to recognizing objects and using language. While children move through this stage at different rates, by the end of the stage all will have obtained, in addition to the traits just mentioned, some new understanding about the world. They will have learned that objects are permanent, that their teddy bears continue to exist even though they may be out of their sight. They will also have learned that to do some things they must *coordinate actions*: to eat from a spoon they need to look at the spoon *and* move the spoon to their mouths. Finally, as an outgrowth of learning to coordinate actions, children begin to recognize *cause and effect relationships*. Their understanding that their actions *cause* something to happen is a vital link in the chain of thought and behavior that allows them to *act intentionally*.

2. Preoperational Thinking

In this stage, which lasts from the end of stage 1 until about the age of seven, physical development—while still impressive—takes a back seat to the advancements children make in their *understanding* of the world. This stage is almost without exception divided by developmentalists into two substages, preconceptual thinking and intuitive thinking. This always leaves me wondering whether all Piaget is divided into four, five, or six parts. Anyhow, the first substage is:

2a. Preconceptual Thinking

In this substage, from about two until four years of age, children are able to devise functional, albeit incomplete, conceptual classes. Hence in this stage all women often become "Mommy," all men "Daddy," all animals "Kitty" or "Doggie" or whatever the dominant species of the household happens to be. It is the incomplete nature of the children's understanding of categories that gives the stage its name: *precon*ceptual.

2b. Intuitive Thinking

In this substage, which ranges from about age four until the end of the preoperational period at about seven, the child's understanding of classes becomes more complete, allowing finer distinctions among classes and categories—only Mommy is Mommy, only Mrs. Hill is the teacher. But the child's thought processes are still dominated by *perception* as opposed to logic. It is from this substage that the diagrams we most often associate with Piaget are taken. A child in this stage will agree that the glasses in Figure A contain an equal amount of fluid. However, that same child, given a choice between the glasses in Figure B—which also contain an equal amount of fluid—will say that the glass on the left contains more fluid because the fluid in the narrow glass rises higher than the fluid in the other glass.

Other characteristics of this substage include an exceptionally egocentric view of the world and a lingering inability to deal with classes within classes—things are either this or that, not this and that.

I could go on and condense the final two stages—if I were writing a book about developmental psychology I would—but it should be clear by now that according to Piaget kids do and understand certain kinds of things at fairly predictable times and in reasonably similar ways. Although Piaget's work, published in French during the 1920s and 1930s, was full of insight, it really did not get much exposure in this country until the 1960s. But when people found out about it, they began to put Piaget's perspective to good use. Among them was Dr. T. Berry Brazelton, noted expert on parenting and child development. It

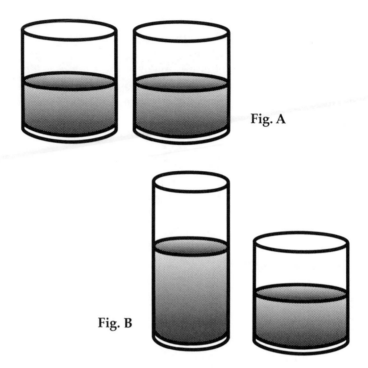

Fig. A

Fig. B

is quite apparent that Brazelton has been strongly influenced by Piaget. But Brazelton, especially in his *Infants and Mothers*, points out what many developmentalists fail to grasp—developmental stages are only general approximations. Yet, if we look at the stages noted above, we can see how someone could create a scheme designed to tell us exactly what our child *should* be doing at any particular time. We've all read the books that tell us things like, "By eleven months your child should be pulling up by herself, standing alone, and walking unsupported for short distances." And there we are with a one-year-old who still likes to crawl backwards, so we hustle off to our long-suffering pediatrician to find out "what's wrong" with our child.

As Dr. Brazelton points out, there is nothing wrong with children who do not fit the pigeon-holed schemes of some strict developmentalists. Children (and parents for that matter) are wonderfully different and complex creatures, and "normal development" only defines average—it has little to do with good or bad, right or wrong, proper or improper. We can see how this perspective on development can allow us to understand our children better by comparing Piaget's stages above with Brazelton's discussion of how different babies do different things at different times. The following paragraphs are taken from

Brazelton's book *Infants and Mothers*, specifically from the chapter in which he discusses five-month-old babies:

Average Baby: Experimentation absorbed Louis' day. Since he could be propped up in a bounce chair for long periods, he had a three-dimensional world to learn about. He found learning an exciting job. His span of attention had increased, and with minor help from his family, he could lie on his back, or sit in his chair for an hour and a half to two hours. He was no longer happy with a mobile or a cradle-gym that was out of reach. He wanted it close enough to feel and examine. He needed to touch, to hold, to turn, to examine, to rattle, to mouth each toy. He was no longer satisfied with just watching—with a two-dimensional approach to a toy. His concepts were now three dimensional, and he screamed with frustration when he could not reach an object. His eyes, fingers, and mouth were integrated as he learned (137).

Quiet Baby: Laura's contentment continued. This contrasted with the build-up of activity in Louis. She handles her developing awareness in an entirely different way. Her sucking on fingers and toys was increasing in intensity, as she lay looking around with wide, knowing eyes. She had learned to bring her feet to her mouth and even sucked on her toes. She also chewed now as she sucked on her thumb. With a toy, she mouthed and chewed on every available edge. As she did, she seemed to savor each separate facet of it. No longer was the soft, red ball her favorite toy. She liked harder objects with corners that were cool to her gums. She transferred a toy easily from one hand to the other and seemed to get pleasure from this. As she took a toy with her right hand, she waved it. Next she transferred it to the left and repeated the same waving gesture—back and forth in repetitious play—one hand imitating the other (147).

Active Baby: Days were not long enough for Daniel. He rushed through them headlong. On his back, he was freest to perform. He rolled and rolled, twisting half his body to pull the upper half over. He rolled to his belly and arched up on his arms to look around. As he looked around from this vantage point, he seemed to digest what he had done, make a decision, and roll back again. There he bent himself forward as if he wanted to come to sit. This continuous activity took up most of Daniel's day. It also spilled over into the night. Whenever he came to semi-consciousness in the night, Daniel rolled himself over in his crib. This activity woke him, and he tried to soothe himself with more activity (151).

Of course, Brazelton's explanations and discussions of each child are much more extensive than these brief quotes, but I think you can see what I'm getting at—three "normal" children manifest very different behaviors at the same age. Developmental stages are approximations of normal and should be viewed that way.

So what does all this have to do with television and our kids? In short, we might be better advised—at least where teaching our kids about TV is concerned—to soft-pedal the Piaget and push Fred Rogers a little more when he tells each of us, "You're special."

I feel this is especially important when we look at the developmental issue in relation to television, because when we mix developmental psychology with television some erroneous assumptions can emerge from otherwise sound research results. For example, a recent study by Alan Ruben of Kent State University indicates that children's preferences for various types of television programs change with age. Kids five to seven prefer cartoons over comedies, as—to a lesser extent—do eight- and nine-year-olds. But kids ten to twelve years old prefer comedies and adult adventure dramas to cartoons. The same study goes on to reveal that young children think that television is "more real" than older children think it is.

The problem with this research lies not in conclusions that the *researchers* draw from it, but rather in the assumptions regarding children and television that *the TV industry and most adults* make on the basis of those conclusions. The assumptions are that cartoons are the natural video fare for children seven and under, and that kids over ten are too sophisticated for cartoons. Similar but differently focused studies lead us to the conclusion that children cannot distinguish between commercials and programs until they cross some mystical developmental barrier, that they must reach a certain age before they can separate reality from fantasy.

Calvin and Hobbes. © 1986 Universal Press Syndicate. Reprinted with permission. All rights reserved.

This conclusion may be an accurate description of *what is*, but I do not believe—as do many people in the business of producing television programs—that it is the way *it has to be*.

Let's suppose that we take a gaggle of four-year-olds to the grocery store and let them shop—without restraint or instruction—for dinner. While we might get some vegetables, and perhaps a fruit or two, the dominant food groups represented would probably be your potato chip and cookie group, your ice cream and candy group, and your Moon Pie and Pepsi group. Were we to shift to a sample of ten- to twelve-year-old shoppers, the level of sugar might drop to allow for the inclusion of your hamburger and hot dog group and your pizza and taco group.

Should our shopping experiment lead us to the conclusion that children must reach a specific developmental stage before they will voluntarily ingest protein or calcium? No, not at all. It should lead us to the conclusion that a lot of us are failing to teach children the basics of good nutrition. The rather skewed food selection is not the result of an inability on the part of the child to organize or understand information about food, as a developmentalist would have it; but rather that the children's exposure to the basics of proper nutrition has been nonexistent, incomplete, or inaccurate. There are, of course, dangers inherent in teaching children about nutrition. It will be a long time before I forget the occasion when I offered to buy ice cream cones for a couple of cherubic five-year-olds and was refused on the basis that ice cream is just "frozen fat." But my friend's daughter cum nutritionist made a point: children can be *taught*, probably much more than we give them credit for, and at a younger age. And what is true for ice cream is also true for the "frozen fats" of television.

So my response to the developmental issue would be to spend as little time as possible worrying about my children's developmental stages and spend as much time as possible teaching them the first two golden rules of television.

Reprinted by permission of UFS, Inc.

Golden Rule of Television Number One: There is a difference between a *character* and a *real person*. I started teaching this rule with "Sesame Street." When Andrea was barely a year and a half old, we would sit and watch the program while playing the "real and character game." When Big Bird came on the screen I would say something like, "Oh! There's Big Bird, he's a puppet—what a lovely character!" And then when Maria came on I would say, "And here comes Maria, she's a real person, she's a woman just like Mommy." And so it would go: as each performer, animal, vegetable, or puppet, played their part I would deem them either real people or characters. I played by myself for the first few months, but soon Andrea began to play along, asking about certain performers, "Is she a real person or a character?" and volunteering information about others, "The cows are puppets, they aren't real." She was soon able to make that important distinction, not only on "Sesame Street," but on most children's programs. This naturally made it easier to teach her **Golden Rule of Television Number Two: There is a difference between *real* and *make-believe*.**

Fred Rogers and his long-running program, "Mister Rogers' Neighborhood," gives us some excellent assistance in teaching our children this rule. "Mister Rogers" contains a regular program segment called the "Neighborhood of Make-Believe." One enters and leaves the Neighborhood of Make-Believe by a very well established ritual. First, Mister Rogers walks over to a set of electric train tracks at one side of his living room and pushes a button while saying something like, "Would you like to go to the Neighborhood of Make-Believe? All right, here comes the trolley."

At this point an electric trolley comes rolling out on its little tracks and stops by Mister Rogers when he pushes the button again. Mister Rogers often demonstrates how he makes the trolley move—"See, I have these buttons here that make the trolley move back and forth"—emphasizing that his program tries to be as real as possible. The trolley is not magic; it is just an electric train, like the one your children may have. Once the trolley has stopped, Mister Rogers asks his viewers what they would like to pretend, or "make believe," is happening in the Neighborhood of Make-Believe today. Rogers then suggests an idea usually having to do with the topic of that day's program or a continuing make-believe story. He pushes the button, and the trolley chugs off down the track and disappears into a tunnel in the wall.

Next we see the trolley emerging from the other end of the tunnel it entered in Mister Rogers's living room, and we know we are in the Neighborhood of Make-Believe. The trolley usually stops in front of the castle of King Friday the 13th, ruler of the Neighborhood of Make-Believe. The neighborhood is populated by puppets and actors playing roles—all *characters* in terms of Golden Rule Number One—who act out the story for the day. When the make-believe is over, the trolley takes us back to the real world of Mister Rogers's house, where Fred Rogers—the Golden Rule Number One *real person*—discusses what happened in Make-Believe and how it can help us live in the real world.

It does not take too many trips to the Neighborhood of Make-Believe for even two- to three-year-olds to begin to understand the differences between television "real" and television "make-believe." And once they understand it on "Mister Rogers' Neighborhood," they can begin to make the transition to other programs, asking and answering the important question—Is that "real" or is that "make-believe?" It is a concept well within a child's grasp and one that apparently has some staying power. One day I was carrying a load of things up to the attic while six-year-old Andrea was coloring and listening to "Mister Rogers." I came down from the attic just in time to see the trolley return to Mister Rogers's living room, and to hear Andrea sigh and remark to no one in particular, "Well, here we are. Back in reality." Chalk one up for Golden Rule Number Two!

Once your child is armed with the ability to understand and utilize the concepts behind the first two golden rules, you are now ready to tackle the second major issue connected with children and television.

The Sex and Violence Issue

This second issue is really two separate issues, but they are often lumped together as one concern, as a matter of fact they are often lumped together as one word, "sexnviolence." I've heard it used for years at television conferences, "What do you think about the sexnviolence issue?" or "How do you think we can best address the concerns arising from sexnviolence on television?" Well, call me an old-fashioned romantic if you will, but I see them as totally separate issues, irreconcilable concepts. Once you add violence to sex it is no longer sex, just a more abusive form of violence. But that is another issue; our concern here is with television programs that feature obviously sexual or obviously violent material, or both. We want to know what their impact is, and we want to know how to deal with them in the context of the family. Well, the first thing that we do is to simply remove from the list of acceptable choices those programs that we, as a family—or as parents—deem objectionable. That is the kernel of our first option in the sexnviolence issue: *control access.*

This is a hard one to enforce, especially with older children, but it is easier once we stop and define some basics again. Free access to television programs is *not* a feature of the Bill of Rights. Children do not have an inalienable right to watch sleazy TV. Given the choice, they will often choose to watch adult programs, but you as a parent are not required to give them that choice. *All* their friends do *not* watch "Dallas," or "Dynasty," or even "St. Elsewhere" or "L.A. Law." There are a lot of programs out there, sleazy and otherwise, that are just not suitable for children. You would not hesitate to control your children's access to substances that might harm them: drugs, alcohol, tobacco, twinkies, etc. You need not hesitate to control their exposure to television programs you deem objectionable either.

I realize there are some problems in this notion of controlling access. And the problems differ as children's ages differ. But in this chapter we are concerned with *children*, preteens, nonadolescents. These are people who have no business watching any of the programs I mentioned above, for two reasons.

The first is that the programs focus on content, relationships, and issues that fall outside the purview of childhood. David Elkind has written an excellent book called *The Hurried Child: Growing Up Too Fast Too Soon*, 2d ed. (Reading, Mass.: Addison-Wesley Publishing Co., 1989), in which he discusses the myriad ways we have devised to strip the luxury of childhood innocence from our children by forcing them into adult roles more and more quickly. By allowing our children to watch adult programming, we force them to address adult issues and concerns before they are intellectually and emotionally ready to do so. That is not to say that they cannot adapt, that they cannot learn about those issues. The world has proved quite adequately that young children *can* "deal with" the harsh realities of divorce, sexual abuse, drug abuse, violence, and hatred. The question we need to address is whether we *want* them to learn about those issues before it is absolutely necessary. And regardless of timing, we need to ask whether we want them to learn about those issues from the slick offerings of commercial television. I think not.

The second reason children should not watch adult programs is that they should be in bed. I cannot believe I just said that, but I did, and I am even a little surprised at how strongly I believe it. But my belief is based on two perspectives. First, I am a teacher. I have taught college students all my adult life. I like to think of myself as a good teacher, an interesting teacher—sometimes as even a charismatic and dynamic teacher. But kids still fall asleep in my classes. I must admit that there are some days when I really do not blame them. Not all aspects of media criticism are fascinating. But I become angry and frustrated when interesting things are going on and a normally bright and attentive student just drops off because he or she can't keep the old peepers open. Sometimes you get an apology—"I had to work late," "It was my roommate's twenty-first birthday," etc.—but the point is that students cannot concentrate and learn when they *need more sleep*.

What is true for the young adults who frequent my classrooms is even more important for young children whose bodies are still pouring huge amounts of energy into simply growing. The difference between children who have slept well and children who have not is truly miraculous. Well-rested children can say "please" and "thank you." Well-rested children can tolerate a reprimand with a cheerful apology. Well-rested children can color and read by themselves. Well-rested children can stop crying. Well-rested children can refrain from making war upon their siblings. I realize that even well-rested children do not necessarily do *all* these lovely things—but a good night's sleep places it within the realm of the possible. For sleep-deprived children, such tasks are far beyond their capabilities.

What we often forget is that the well-rested child and the sleep-deprived child are two residents of the same body. A child often fights the prompting of his or her own body's call for sleep, especially when lured by the glossy high-energy allure of adult prime-time programs. Do your child a favor; help the well-rested child win the battle for your child's mind and body and get her or him in bed at a reasonable hour.

I realize that "reasonable hour" is a very flexible concept. Our six-year-old has a bedtime of seven o'clock on school nights and eight on week-ends. Obviously, both those get compromised on occasion and adjusted for summer; but they are targets that both parent and child understand and, when hit, they make for a well-rested child. Look at your family's schedule, set some targets for your "reasonable hour," and stick to your guns! Perhaps the most important concept about bedtime, at least from the perspective of this book, is that it is *never* extended for high-energy prime-time television. If you make this mistake you are probably exposing your children to television programs they would be better off without and keeping them up past their bedtimes—guaranteeing yourself grumpy company the next morning.

No, I do not know why the networks insist on airing holiday specials for four-, five-, and six-year-olds at eight or nine o'clock. It is just another one of their many ways of showing us they do not really care about audience members, only about the commercials we watch. So what do you do if your children just *have* to watch "It's the Great Pumpkin Charlie Brown!" which comes on after bedtime? Tape it for viewing at a more suitable hour. If that is not possible, then make an afternoon nap, or at least an extended quiet time, the price for viewing the postbedtime treat (pajamas on first and bed right after goes without saying).

Our second option on the sex and violence issue is to make sure that

we *define values.* How we as parents define our attitudes about sex and violence is going to have a great influence upon how our children come to understand those dynamic concepts. Any swift review of human history will reveal that people's attitudes about sex, and about the use of force in conflict, are as varied as humankind itself. And I certainly have no intention of telling you where your family should stand on those issues. But what I am suggesting—very strongly—is that you make sure your child knows where *you* stand on these issues. Let's look at the issues of sex and violence one at a time, because for preteens, television should address the issues separately, if at all.

Sex

If you follow the control access game plan carefully, sex on television really should not be much of a problem for children in the "McKids Clothes" age range (infants to six or seven). "It's Your First Kiss Charlie Brown" is about as racy as it should get. This issue is of much more concern with adolescents and older children who are discovering their sexuality in relationships and are unsure about how sex and relationships go together. And we will address those concerns in the next chapter, "Growing up on the River."

However, we cannot control access to television completely, and it is vital that we realize two important issues about young children and sex. Let's consider a program for kids in this age range that allows us to examine both issues, "The Berenstain Bears' Easter Surprise." In this program Mama Bear's lap disappears when she is pregnant with Sister Bear and reappears after Sister is born. In one early scene Brother Bear asks, "What happened to Mama's lap?" Papa Bear—as is his wont—grins foolishly and changes the subject. Later in the program, after Sister has been born, Brother Bear asks directly, "Papa, where did the baby come from?" Papa bravely responds, "Uh, that one's for your mother." Mother Bear takes Brother up on her reconstructed lap and says, referring to a song from earlier in the program, "Do you remember about the robins? And the miracle of birth? Well . . ." At which point Brother interrupts with, "Mama! Your lap is back!" The narrator intones, "And so it was." We break to a song and the program ends.

The first important issue that the program raises is that no information is better than misinformation. Papa Bear, like many parents, is uncomfortable discussing sex and reproduction with his young son. So he chooses to avoid the issue. This is not the best choice, but it is far better than giving misinformation. Most people try to tell the truth to children, but there is a tendency to hedge when it comes to sex. There are many highly educated, professional, truthful people who are totally honest with their children about every aspect of their lives except sex. And in that area—instead of going with Papa Bear's no information option, they tell their children outrageous things: "Daddy gave Mommy something special to eat and it made a baby in her tummy." The problem is that—when your lie is inevitably discovered—you have taught your kids two bad things. First, you have taught them not to trust you as a source of information regarding sex. Second, and potentially more damaging, you have taught them that *even if you tell the truth about everything else* it is acceptable to lie about sex.

Which brings us to the second important issue about children and sex: Accurate information is better than no information. Our policy has always been to tell the truth when you could, and to tell nothing when the truth seemed inappropriate for discussion with that particular kid at that particular point in time. But that leads us to another question. How do you tell the truth? What words do you use to tell your little Brother Bears "where the baby came from?" And how do we know what truth is important when?

Most of the time parents do not have the Berenstain Bears' option of breaking to a song and ending the show. They have to come up with answers, which ideally should be consistent with the values of the household. It is clearly beyond the scope of this book to provide such answers, but fortunately for tongue-tied parents everywhere, the question, Where did the baby come from?, is the central concern of a number of excellent books. You might want to check one of the following out of your local library:

Raising a Child Conservatively in a Sexually Permissive World, by Sol Gordon and Judith Gordon. New York: Simon and Schuster, 1983.
Talking with Your Child about Sex, by Drs. Mary Calderone and James W. Ramey. New York: Random House, 1982.

Getting Closer: Discover and Understand Your Child's Secret Feelings about Growing Up, by Ellen Rosenberg. New York: Berkley Publishing Co., 1985.

If the library does not have them, any good bookstore can order them for you. In addition to these books for parents of children from one through sixteen, there are lots of good books out there for the children themselves, for example, *Where Did I Come From?*, by Peter Mayle (Secaucus, N.J.: Lyle Stuart, 1973). So look around, it's a brave new world on the shelves of your local library and bookstore.

Violence

Without a doubt, violence causes the greatest concern among parents of young children. Visions of Wiley Coyote flattened under huge boulders dance in our heads, and we are afraid that our children will act out those visions in the living room, on the playground, in the classroom, and eventually in the Home for Terminally Incorrigible Children.

Calvin and Hobbes. © 1988 Universal Press Syndicate. Reprinted with permission. All rights reserved.

As usual there are grounds for concern. Unlike sex, violence has become a staple of children's television and cannot be simply eliminated. There is a very simple reason for that, a reason that is tied to the central structure of drama: conflict. All drama is based on some sort of conflict; if there is no conflict there is no plot, no action, no interest. And then, of course, there must be a resolution of the conflict. Good guys have to win, bad guys have to lose.

The problem most parents encounter is that resolution in children's television often occurs through some sort of physical mayhem. And they worry that the modeling of that mayhem will lead to the violent, aggressive behavior that eventually gets children into trouble with the law, or at least makes them persona non grata at the better birthday parties in the neighborhood and at grandmother's house. However, the jury is still out on that question. As Robert M. Liebert and Joyce Sprafkin point out in their excellent book *The Early Window: Effects of Television on Children and Youth* (New York: Pergamon, 1988), it seems fairly clear that there is a strong link between watching violent television and increased aggressiveness in children. But they also point out that television is only *a* cause, not *the* cause; there is no *one* cause of aggressive behavior in children (161).

Nonetheless, these findings demonstrate again that we need to use some common sense as we provide guidelines for television viewing for young children. We need to remember that any kind of television in excess is not good for children—if for no other reason than it squeezes out beneficial activities like reading and playing outside. But limiting exposure to specific types of television moves a bit beyond that basic idea. In the section above we discussed limiting a young child's access to the sexually explicit messages of adult television for the simple reason that such messages should have no place in the world of childhood. On the other hand, we acknowledged that even very good programs for children often lead to questions about sexuality and reproduction. And we discussed the advisability of answering those questions as honestly as possible—both to maintain our credibility for later, more in-depth discussions, and to prevent misinformation and neighborhood mythology from becoming a significant part of our children's sex education.

If you stop and think about it for a moment that really is just another application of the two golden rules of television we have already talked about: There is a difference between *characters* and *real people*; and there is a difference between *real* and *make-believe*. Those same rules will stand us in good stead as we follow three steps designed to deal with the dominant presence of violence in children's television.

First, we control access by limiting the amount of time a child can spend watching TV—all types of TV. You can do this on the basis of hours per day or hours per week. It really does not matter as long as you make it stick within reasonable limits. You might want to put a chart up next to the TV to record what programs your child has chosen to watch and to mark off the hours of the viewing allotment that have been used up.

Second, we encourage our kids to watch "good" programs, both by subtle means—"Oh, yeah, that sounds neat. Maybe we'll make some popcorn and watch it together,"—and by overt bribery—"If you don't

Sample Viewing Chart

Time	Monday 3 hrs	Tuesday 3 hrs	Wednesday 3 hrs	Thursday 3 hrs	Friday 4 hrs	Saturday 4 hrs
0:00 hrs						
:30	4:30 - 5:00 Cosby ch. 5	ET: tape	4:30 - 5:00 Cosby ch. 5			
1:00	5:30 - 6:00 ch. 5 Punky Brewster		5:30 - 6:00 ch. 5 Punky Brewster			
1:30	7:00 - 8:00		Square one tapes			
2:00	Animal World ch. 4	4:30 - 5:00 Cosby ch. 5	From Mon. & Tues			
2:30	Tape: Nova	5:30 - 6:00 ch. 5 Punky Brewster				
3:00						
3:30		Remember: Tape Square One				
4:00	Remember: Tape Square One ch. 4 5:00 PM					

Sample TV Viewing Chart Showing Programs and Viewing Limits

watch 'Captain Power' this week, I'll let you watch an extra hour of programs we agree are OK." (Sometimes you do what works right now and worry about damage control later.)

Third, and this is very important, we keep our children company during those conflict-laden programs they are loath to desert, and we flail about with the two golden rules of television as we go. "Oh, look. Here come those cartoon monsters again. I'm really glad that they're *just characters* in a program and *not real people*." And, "Wow! Did you see how he punched that guy out? Good thing this is *just make-believe*. If people behaved that way *in real life* they'd spend the whole day on the time-out chair."

It is vital that we maintain step three, that we continue to emphasize—as often as we can stand to, and as long as the kids might possibly be listening—that television is not real, that the behaviors that *characters* demonstrate in *make-believe* situations are different from the behaviors that *real people* are expected to demonstrate in *real life*.

Violence on the News

The first two golden rules of television raise a difficult but important issue—what about television that does talk about real life? What about violence on the news? Joshua Meyrowitz describes his young daughter's reaction to a news report of an airplane accident in which all the passengers, except for one little girl, were killed. "I don't ever want to watch the news again!" she said. "I don't want to hear about people getting dead." Meyrowitz goes on to say, "It's no surprise that the plane-crash story would greatly disturb my daughter, for she and the newly orphaned Cecilia are both the same age—just four years old" ("Is TV Keeping Us *Too* Well-Informed?," *TV Guide*, January 9, 1988).

There is another reason for the child's distress, one that goes beyond the notion of age mates. Meyrowitz's daughter, not surprisingly for the daughter of a media critic, had been taught the first two golden rules of television. She knew the difference between characters and real people, and she knew the difference between the real world and make-believe. She knew that real people had died on that crash and that a real little girl no longer had a Mommy or Daddy to hug her and put her to bed. No wonder she was upset.

Patricia Palmer's *The Lively Audience* suggests another reason for children's distress about violence in the news. She asserts that children have come to understand violence as a story element. They realize that violence—be it fists, guns, or death rays—is often part of the climax of a story. But, she goes on to say, "Violence on the news, because it did not happen in the framework of a story which gave it meaning, was often disturbing from a child's perspective" (126).

So do we attempt to control our children's access to the news? Meyrowitz and Palmer waffle on their advice. Palmer says, "Because of the high priority adults place on television news, they do not seem to recognize that for children this may be one of the most disturbing forms of television violence" (127). That seems to speak out for controlling access to viewing. But Meyrowitz seems to imply that the "high priority" (to use Palmer's words) that parents give to news overrides the need to protect children from the impact of news violence. In *No Sense of Place*, the book upon which the *TV Guide* article is based, Meyrowitz says, "Many children are exposed to adult news . . . because their parents watch the news during dinner. To control children's television viewing, therefore, parents must either limit their own viewing or physically divide the family" (246). He repeats the point in the *TV Guide* article: "And if the whole family is in one room, we can't censor our children's viewing without censoring our own. As a result, television takes our children across the globe even before we give them permission to cross the street" (5).

True—but only if we chose *not* to censor our viewing. Only if we chose to allow television to walk our children through the rapes, wrecks, and riots of the evening news. That is not our only option. We can, and in my opinion should, censor our own viewing to avoid exposing our children to the random violence of the evening news.

The Palmer study, the Meyrowitz article, and common sense all argue against showing children televised portrayals of adults killing each other, plane crashes, car wrecks, and other examples of cultural mayhem that have come to pass as journalism on the tube. But Meyrowitz raises the question of the inconvenience that arises for adults who trim their news viewing in the interests of their children.

Choosing to skip the evening news demonstrates—at a very minimal level—your willingness to sacrifice the convenience of the six o'clock news for your children's well-being. And if you discuss with your children the idea that you are choosing not to watch television news because it shows too much violence, you are modeling for them the kind of selective consumption of television that you hope they will demonstrate in their own viewing.

I am not suggesting that parents restrict their intake of television to those programs that are suitable for their children. But I am suggesting that we can—without reducing our intake—restructure our consumption of news in several ways.

1. Switch to a late-evening newscast. Local news stations tend to give their most comprehensive coverage on their final newscasts anyhow.

2. If you have a VCR, tape your favorite national "dinnertime" news for viewing when the kids have gone to bed.

3. Subscribe to a national newspaper such as the *New York Times,* the *Los Angeles Times,* or the *Washington Post.* There are a lot of good ones out there that will give you more and better information than the best of television news. The same usually goes for most daily "hometown" papers, unless they are completely dominated by "chicken dinner circuit" items of exclusively local interest.

4. Subscribe to a TV cable system that carries CNN, or "CNN Headline News," which gives you access to a news program whenever you wish to watch it.

I am sure you can come up with other ways to get the news without exposing the kids to what is basically just a headline service with pictures—pictures and stories that are often quite disturbing to young children.

Before we move on to the third issue raised by the children and TV brouhaha, I do want to mention another problem that seems to walk hand-in-hand with the issue of sex and violence on television. That problem is the use of alcohol and, to a lesser extent these days, tobacco on television—prime-time programming in particular. It seems as though any successful person out there in Televisionland has an office with a bar. Deals, celebrations, and seductions are all hastened with some alcoholic potion or another. Along the same line, moments of significant stress are often eased with a cigarette, many times driving the main characters back to a habit they had tried to quit.

It is obvious that these scenes do not grossly distort society—a lot of folks in America smoke and drink. My concern is that the scenes tend to glamorize behaviors that are problems in our society. I think I can truthfully say that all the smokers I know today would like to be able to stop. I know I do not want to start again. I still like a cold beer on a hot summer afternoon, and a nice wine does add to those rare dinners when my wife and I sneak off on our own. But again, the concern is television's tendency to glamorize behaviors that are not very good for any of us and can be deadly to some. My point is simply that the use of alcohol and tobacco is another area—along with sex and violence— that needs our attention and monitoring.

Commercials

Of the three issues that make up the brouhaha of children's television, we encounter this one most often. As the first chapter pointed out, television is first and foremost a business, and commercials are the bread and butter of that business. Unfortunately, in recent years the television industry has intensified its children's marketing strategy. Wise parents counter the kid-commercial onslaught with **Golden Rule of Television Number Three:** *Commercials* **are different from** *programs.*

Like the first two golden rules of television, the third rule needs to be taught early and often. One problem is that in order to teach kids about commercials you need to watch commercials designed for children, which may be much more difficult than giving up the six o'clock news.

There are a couple of kid's shows on commercial networks that can make teaching this rule fun. I mention only a couple because—since we want to teach this rule early—we are restricted to programs that will hold the attention of toddlers. "Today's Special," carried in my market on the Nickelodeon cable channel, was one of Andrea's favorites from the very beginning of her viewing history, and deservedly so. It has a nice blend of human and puppet characters, treats one "special" topic each day, and is strong on music. "Today's Special" is produced by a group called the Ontario Television Workshop, based in Ontario, Canada, but you might also check locally produced programs for kids—some good ones pop up every once in a while.

The commercial broadcast networks do not really offer much for toddlers, but there are some choices that work well for the preschool set, as well as their older siblings. "Jim Henson's Muppet Babies" is a genuinely creative, entertaining program, as is "Pee-Wee's Playhouse," a sort of "David Letterman" for those six and under.

Ahyhow, the object is to sit down with your child and watch some of these programs following the first two golden rules about real people versus characters and the real world versus make-believe. But then when a commercial comes along you introduce a new line of remarks like, "Oh, here comes a commercial! This is different from the rest of the program, isn't it?"

Depending on the age of the child, you can expand on the basic difference between commercials and programs in different ways. For the very young child you can simply distinguish between the two forms: "See? Those are different characters from the ones we were just watching. That's a bunny rabbit character trying to grab the cereal from the little boy and girl characters—isn't that silly? Bunnies don't eat cereal in real life. Oh, good, the commercial is over. Now we can get back to our story."

As the child gets a little older you can shift your emphasis a bit: "Oh, another commercial, I wonder what they want us to go spend our money on now? It's that plastic doll again, remember, the one that broke so easily? We certainly won't waste our money on that, will we?"

And then, of course, comes that time when Mom and Dad suddenly go brain dead and are reduced to asking questions: "What are they selling? What does it cost? Really? How long would it take you to save for that on your allowance? Wouldn't you rather go to a good college?" You get the idea, let the kids think they're teaching you.

As with the first two golden rules, the idea behind the third golden rule is to break up the image of "television as reality." As parents we need to show our children that television is a storytelling machine, and that it has its own reasons for telling stories. Commercials are one kind of television story, and the reason television shows us commercials is to persuade us to buy goods and services. We need to teach our children that we do not need most of those goods and services; that commercials, while often amusing, moving, and entertaining, are only there to separate us from our money. We need to teach our children that advertisers have stopped just pushing their products as products and have started to persuade us that those products somehow manifest values, lifestyles, even success and self-worth. We need to combat that onslaught, and the first line of defense is that third golden rule of television.

Reprinted by permission of Universal Press Syndicate, Inc.

The Sneaky Sell: Program-Length Commercials

There's a new wrinkle in teaching Golden Rule Number Three. Sometimes commercials *are not* different from programs. Remember

"Winky Dink"? Well, for those of you who missed him the first time around, I understand he made something of a comeback on the Disney Channel. Anyhow, he was a little character who used to run around on a Saturday morning cartoon and get into terrible fixes from which only you could rescue him—if you had a Winky Dink Kit. A Winky Dink Kit consisted of a piece of greenish plastic that you would rub onto the TV screen. The kit also contained a big black crayon, and when Winky Dink got stuck on one side of the river with the bad guys chasing him, you took your crayon and drew a line across the river. Winky scurried across the river and you erased the line before the bad guys could follow. Now, admittedly, watching Winky Dink took an act of faith; we closed our eyes to the fact that Winky would run across the river even if we didn't draw the bridge. We ignored the fact that the bad guys wouldn't follow even if we left the bridge intact. And our parents would try to overlook the times when we drew on the screen ·without the benefit of the Winky Dink Plastic Screen. But the most amazing thing about Winky Dink was the stuff he didn't have.

When you walked into a toy store, sometimes you could find a Winky Dink Kit. But that was it, no Winky Dink dolls, or action figures, or castles, or Dink blasters or anything. That is certainly a far cry from today when you walk into any toy store and find yourself surrounded by all the inhabitants of children's television. That is largely the result of the "program-length commercial."

Program-length commercials are, according to the Federal Communications Commission (FCC), "programs that interweave 'noncommercial' program content so closely with the commercial message that the entire program must be considered commercial." And until the early 1980s they were illegal, based on the FCC's opinion that "[children are] far more trusting of and vulnerable to commercial 'pitches' than are adults."

But in 1981 President Reagan appointed Mark Fowler chairman of the FCC, and Chairman Fowler and He-Man came marching into children's television bringing the big toy companies with them. Unlike his predecessors, who saw the FCC as an agency that had a specific and exceptional obligation to safeguard America's children from unfair broadcasting practices, Fowler believed that "television is just another appliance . . . a toaster with pictures." Armed with this electrifying insight, Fowler set out to deregulate all commercial programming, striking down in the process all regulations regarding commercials in children's television.

Enter He-Man and the "barter deal." A barter deal, of which He-Man was the first, works like this:

1. A toy company develops a product, like the He-Man action figure.
2. In conjunction with a TV production company the toy company develops a television program starring the product.
3. The toy company *gives* the program to a broadcaster or group of broadcasters in return for a couple of minutes of advertising time somewhere else in the children's programming schedule.

It is not too difficult to see why both the toy companies and the broadcasters are so fond of this arrangement. The broadcasters get free programming for the traditionally unprofitable children's viewing slots. Hence, *any* commercials they sell in those time periods are pure profit. In exchange, the toy makers get to air half-hour-long commercials to pitch their line of toys.

Who loses? The toy companies would have us believe that no one does, but sit down some Saturday morning and watch a few of these program-length commercials and I think you will agree that our children are the real losers. The stories come, not from the musings of some modern Hans Christian Andersen, but rather from the "creative departments" of the toy companies. As such, one can guess that the story line will be primarily concerned with the presentation of existing toys and the opportunities to create new ones.

But this symbiotic relationship between toy makers, program producers, and broadcasters does more than merely limit the available stories, it cheapens the child's whole interaction with fantasy. Bruno Bettelheim, the renowned child psychologist, says in his book *The Uses of Enchantment: The Meaning and Importance of Fairy Tales* (New York: Knopf, 1976): "For a story to truly hold the child's attention, it must entertain him and arouse his curiosity. But to *enrich* [emphasis added] his life it must stimulate his imagination; help him to develop his intellect and to clarify his emotions; be attuned to his anxieties and aspirations; give full recognition to his difficulties, while at the same time suggesting solutions to the problems that perturb him."

These are creative and literary tasks that lie far beyond the abilities of the product-restricted stories and programs that currently dominate children's television. As a result, we tend to get junk programs to finance children's television just as the corporate world used to use junk bonds to finance some of its more questionable ventures.

What is the best way to handle these programs? Fall back to the third golden rule, programs and commercials *are too* different, and consult page 56, which identifies the toys featured in programs that are actually commercials.

Because children's toy-based programs are not affected as much by ratings as they are by shifts in the toy market, the lineup of shows

*Partial Listing of Toys That Have Been Turned
into TV Shows since the 1982–83 Season*

Bionic Six
The Biskitts
The Blinkins
BraveStarr
Cabbage Patch Kids
Captain Power and the
  Soldiers of the
  Future
Care Bears
Centurions
The Charmkins
Donkey Kong
Donkey Kong Jr.
Dungeons and Dragons
Force III
Frogger
The Future
The Get Along Gang
• G.I. Joe: A Real American
  Hero
Glo Friends
Gobots
Golden Girl
He-Man and the Masters of
  the Universe
Hello Kitty
Herself the Elf
Hugga Bunch
Inhumanoids
• Jayce and the Wheeled
  Warriors
Jem
The Kindles
Lady Lovely Locks and the
  Pixietails
Lazer Tag
M.A.S.K.
Mapletown
Monchichis
Moon Dreamers
Ms. Pacman

My Little Pony
My Pet Monster
Pacman
Photon
Pitfall
Poochie
Popples
Pound Puppies
Q*Bert
Rainbow Brite
Robo Force
Robotech
Robotix
Rock Lords
Rose Petal Place
Rubik the Amazing Cube
Saber Rider and the Star
Sheriffs
Scrabble People
Sectaurs
She-Ra, Princess of Power
The Shirt Tales
SilverHawks
The Snorks
Snuggles the Seal
Spiral Zone
Star Fairies
Strawberry Shortcake
Supernaturals
Sweet Pea
Sylvanian Families
Teddy Ruxpin
The Transformers
ThunderCats
TigerSharks
Tranzor-Z
Visionaries
Voltron, Defender of the
  Universe
Vytor the Starfire Champion
The Wuzzles

shifts quickly sometimes. There are probably programs on the list that are no longer with us, and undoubtedly new ones have been added. But even this partial list of sixty-two toy-based programs is pretty appalling. So what are you supposed to do, not let your kids watch *any* of them? That would be my preference, and is my advice, but even a guy with a cause occasionally retains some common sense. I know you're going to let your kids watch some of these shows. I know my kids are going to watch them, too, because the sheer number of them makes them hard to avoid. But let's do two things. First, let's make sure that we, and our kids, keep in mind the fact that we are watching commercials with the same objective as other commercials: they want to sell us toys, but they are too sneaky to come out and admit it. Second, let's try to change the current state of children's television by supporting strong guidelines for commercials in children's programming. Some good people have already taken significant steps in this direction, and we would be well-advised to walk along with them. I will talk more about this issue in Chapter 5, "You and Me against the World," but for now let me just reemphasize what I feel is the most important idea in this rather long chapter: *You can control television's impact on your children.*

Given all the things I have asked you to consider doing in this chapter I realize that, at first blush, it seems as though you will spend more time taking care of your kids' television habits than doing anything else. That is only true for a little while. It's like learning to drive a standard-shift vehicle. The first time you do it, it seems like an endless string of complex tasks—make sure you are in neutral and the parking brake is off, turn on the ignition, check behind you, depress the clutch, step on the brake, shift into reverse, release the brake, give it some gas, gently let out the clutch, back out of the drive, let up on the gas, depress the clutch, step on the brake, shift into first, release the brake, give it some gas, let up on the clutch—and you jerked off down the street into the adult world of driving. Now you can do all that without waking up—a very bad idea—but something we often catch ourselves doing.

Starting your children on the right road to wise television usage is the same sort of process—it seems difficult and complex at first, but you will be amazed how fast they can pick up good viewing habits. Believe me, it is worth the effort.

4

Growing Up on the River: Adolescents and Television

There is some mystical relationship between children and rivers, and while Mark Twain was not the only author to explore this relationship, he was certainly one of the best. As he led us along the mighty Mississippi with Tom Sawyer and Huckleberry Finn, he was able to capture the essential differences in the ways children, adolescents, and adults see rivers.

Children see rivers as magical kingdoms. Every overhanging tree limb is a precarious bridge to be traversed. Every rock becomes a castle to breach or to defend. Every nook or sheltered eddy begs to be a pirate's landing. From early morning mist, through midday sun, past evening's hush, into the black and silver moonlight of night—rivers are kingdoms for children.

Adults bring to rivers the varied perceptions that accompany things adult. For some adults rivers are to be bridged, or dammed, or channeled; they are obstacles subdued in pursuit of goals or profits. To other adults rivers are commodities to be packaged, marketed, displayed, and publicized with powerboats and skis, or balloons, hot dogs, and beer. And finally there is that group of adults for whom rivers mean solitude, who rest their harried psyches in the calm, steady peacefulness of flowing water—fishing, floating, dozing, and dreaming.

Although it is true that Tom and Huck often saw themselves as the most feared pirates ever to prowl the Mississippi, and although they spent a good deal of time fishing, floating, dreaming, and dozing, in the end they saw the river neither as children nor as adults see it, but as all adolescents come to see rivers—as highways to their dreams. For an adolescent a river runs not from upstream to downstream, not from above the bend to below it, but from today into tomorrow, from the rather boring present into all the marvelous possibilities of the future.

Television is an electronic river for the adolescents of today. In place of riverboat captains puffing pipes and telling tales of the world around the bend, TV's news and dramas import moving visions of hundreds of potential tomorrows. The riverboat gambler gives way to "Wheel of Fortune," "The Dating Game," and "Win, Lose or Draw." The patent medicine huckster steps aside for Madison Avenue's slicker sell, and the player piano is overwhelmed by MTV. But the lure of moving waters still remains, for adolescents see television—as they see rivers—differently than do children and adults.

In the last chapter, we discussed the fact that with children our main television concerns are teaching them the difference between real and make-believe, helping them to distinguish between programs and commercials, and protecting them from programs that simply fall outside the realm of childhood. Adolescents, particularly young adolescents, present a very different set of concerns.

Young adolescents understand that television is not "reality," they understand that the dramas are fiction, that the commercials are there to sell products, that Geraldo is 90 percent hype and 10 percent information. But the paradox is that they do not believe—completely—that television is not "reality." It truly is like a river—a parade of possible tomorrows running from their rather boring present into a technicolor, high-definition, stereophonic future. Our job is to help them navigate that river, avoid the sandbars, run the rapids, and lend a hand at the portage around the falls—at least whenever we can.

One thing that makes the task of navigation easier is that while we treat them differently with young adolescents, the three major issues are still there and the golden rules of television still apply. So let's look at the river that way.

Developmental Concerns

With the little ones we were concerned that they wouldn't "be ready" for certain kinds of messages. It was frustrating, yet somehow comforting as well. They still needed us, we still had to protect them. But even Piaget says that we have to let go of part of that idea now. Children over eleven years old are grouped with adults in the formal operational period. They have all the tools they are going to get for making sense of the world around them. But don't get me wrong, that doesn't mean that we give our kids 'twixt twelve and twenty a hearty pat on the back and send them down the river alone. This is when it can really get tough, giving them help when they most need it and least want it. They have the tools to make sense of the world, but they have not had much experience with the task at hand. I mean you could turn me loose in the finest service bay in the most fully equipped automobile dealership in the city; I *still* couldn't do more than change tires, spark plugs, oil, and light bulbs.

The main problem is that television exposes young people to a dizzying array of possible beliefs, attitudes, values, and lifestyles all presented as equally plausible models for imitation. Young adolescents spend a good deal of their time trying to figure out what models—from home, school, religious organization, peers, *and* television—are the right ones to imitate. Television is not the model they will usually choose to emulate. Teens are a notoriously bad television market; you know that because you are the one who has to drive them to all those things that they are doing instead of watching television. But if we as parents do not provide teenagers with appropriate models, television will rush in to fill the vacuum.

In order to prevent this vacuum from occurring, we need to remain present in our children's lives. We need to help them process the experiences that life brings to them. And that is true for both real experiences and the experiences they share through television.

In order to help our children interpret the role models presented by television, we can simply refocus the first two golden rules of television that we used when they were younger: There is a difference between a *character* and a *real person*; and there is a difference between *real* and *make-believe*.

With young adolescents we focus our attention on the situations and behaviors and motivations of the people that television presents to us. While we—and our kids—realize that the dramas of television present us with fictions, we must also realize that those fictions present dramatized visions of reality. As such we can use them as situations that allow us to examine and clarify the values that we hold as a family. So we come up with **Adolescent and Adult Corollary to Golden Rules One and Two: Behaviors of characters in television dramas *can and should* be judged by the standards we apply to our own behaviors.**

How do we do that? Well, I suggest we do it by applying the "Media Probe." The Media Probe is a method of encouraging people to sit down as a family and talk about the values that lie behind the behaviors of television characters. The key phrase in that last sentence is "sit down as a family and talk." It is amazing how many parents I talk to who have a hard time recalling the last time they sat down and talked to their adolescent children. The problem seems to be that there is little common ground for young adolescents and adults; conversations when they do occur are often motivated by differences and hence immediately become confrontational. The Media Probe helps overcome a couple of those problems. Since it is a method for examining specific television programs, the programs provide common ground, common experiences. Second, since the discussions center on the behavior of program characters—and not family members—the potential for direct confrontation is reduced. The Media Probe is based on several basic premises regarding television. Let's look at them one at a time.

Media Probe Premise 1: All television programs follow a dramatic structure. It doesn't matter whether we are talking about a sitcom, a dramatic serial, a soap opera, the news, a documentary, a cartoon, the NCAA Tournament, or a commercial, all television messages tend to be dramas with openings, rising action, climaxes, and resolutions. We will take advantage of this structure as we use the Media Probe.

Media Probe Premise 2: All television examines behaviors in relationships. Again, from "Cosby" to "Miami Vice" to "Wheel of Fortune" to "The Evening News" to a McDonald's commercial, the messages of television reveal how people or institutions behave in relationships, relationships with other people or institutions. With the Media Probe we will isolate relationships of particular importance to us as viewers.

Media Probe Premise 3: As viewers we assign motives to the behaviors that people on television display. We cannot help assigning motives to behaviors on television—otherwise television has no meaning. J. R. wants to divorce Sue Ellen so that he can marry Kimberly Crider, get control of Westar, and get Ewing Oil's name back. The anchorperson asks tough questions because the public deserves answers. Bobby Knight throws a chair because he thinks an official made a bad call. Teenagers wear Levi's 501 jeans so that the other teenagers will like and accept them. We may not assign the same, or even similar, motives to television behaviors as our children do—but we all assign motives.

Media Probe Premise 4: The motives we assign to behaviors on television are based on values. The direct motive for a behavior stems from the character's belief system. J. R. behaves the way he does because *success in business* and the *memory of his father* are more important to him than anything else in the world. The anchorperson thinks the public deserves an answer because he or she believes that *truth and honesty* are mandatory in creating *an informed citizenry* upon which *a democracy* is built. Bobby Knight throws a chair because he believes the official's call might unfairly prevent his team from *winning, and winning* is extremely important to him. Teenagers wear Levi's 501 jeans because *having friends* and *being popular* affirm an adolescent's often shaky self-concept.

Those, then, are the four premises that underlie the Media Probe. I should also point out that there are really several versions of the Media Probe. The one I am going to discuss right now is the version to be used at home with twelve- to fifteen-year-olds. The high school through early college version appears in an appendix at the end of the book. I include it because a lot of young people enjoy the Media Probe as a game. If your kids fit that category, you might want to use the more complicated version. But on to the home-use version.

The intent of the probe is to make the four premises obvious to the whole family, and in doing so begin discussions that will allow us all to see what the program being probed is saying.

Step 1

We want to freeze the content. A number of studies indicate that we have a tendency to forget what we saw in a particular program only moments after the program is over. We can avoid this by mapping the dramatic structure we talked about in Media Probe Premise 1. The easiest way to do this is to turn a sheet of paper on its side and fold it into quarters. We then label the four columns we have created as follows: What's what?—What's going on?—The High Point—Now What? Everybody who watches the program being probed fills in the columns.

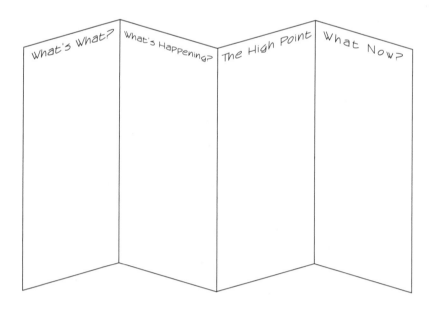

What's What? In this column we write down what we know about the characters and the situation of the program. For example, if we were doing a "Cosby" episode we might write down: "Characters are: Cliff, the father—a doctor; Claire, the mother—a lawyer. Rudy—about six, Vanessa—junior high, Theo—high school. Denise and Sandra away at college. Cliff's office is in the basement."

What's Happening? In this column we write down what happens in the program. In our example we might write: "Show opens with Cliff teaching Rudy to ride her bike. She's wearing pads and a helmet. Next Ms. Westlake, Theo's math teacher, arrives. She's one of Cliff's patients and is expecting a baby any day. Theo and his friend Cockroach come home to study for Ms. Westlake's math test the next day. Vanessa is getting a pimple in the middle of her forehead. Cockroach wants to quit studying. Theo keeps pushing, but Cockroach doesn't think he'll ever need math, because he's going to inherit his dad's scrap metal business. Cliff points out why he will need math in the real world."

The High Point. In this column we write down the climactic moments in the program, those points at which the major plot line or plot lines are resolved. Our example might read: "Ms. Westlake has her baby. The kids in the math class begin to hassle the substitute—at which point Cockroach gets up and tells them that they owe it to Ms. Westlake to behave properly. Rudy learns to ride her bike."

Now What? In this column we describe what happens in the epilogue, the short segment at the end of the program that ties up the loose ends. In this example we might write: "Ms. Westlake's math class goes to take her a card at the hospital to say thank you for being their teacher. She asks Cockroach to stay after the other kids leave. She thanks him for what he said in class."

Step 2

Now that we have frozen the content of the program, we want to examine the other three media probe premises—those that deal with relationships, assigning motives to behaviors, and values. I have found that one good way to get at those issues is to ask a series of four questions:

Question 1. Which of the characters in the program would you most like to spend time with? To have as a friend?

Question 2. What did the character do that makes you think he or she would be a nice friend?

Answering and discussing these questions allow us to share our feelings as a family about the values that hold our family together, as well as to examine how we might behave as a result of those values. Would it be nice to have a friend like Theo who would help you study even when you really did not feel like it? Would it be nice to have a teacher who makes you learn? Does school teach you things you can "really" use? Should Ms. Westlake stay home with her baby, or come back to work?

Question 3. Which of the characters in the program would you *least* like to spend time with? To have as a friend?

Question 4. What did he or she do to make you feel this way?

The answers to these questions allow us to identify behaviors and attitudes that are not acceptable, or are at least distasteful, to various members of the family.

I think it is very important, when discussing these four questions, to include the question Why? Why did Rudy have to wear pads and helmet to ride her bike, even after she could do it? Why did the kids act up in class? Why did Theo want to encourage Cockroach to study? These questions allow us to get at the beliefs and values that underlie behavior, and that relationship between beliefs, values, and behavior is a very important one for young adolescents to understand.

As I am sure you can imagine, members of the family can come up with different results in the Media Probe because they may see different values reflected in the program and disagree on what motivates a character to do something. Disagreements are fine, because they can stimulate lively discussions—discussions that allow us to clarify as a family how we feel we each should behave, and why we believe we should behave that way. The Media Probe can create opportunities for our children to ask us questions they might not otherwise ask or offer explanations they might not otherwise feel comfortable giving.

I have never had any trouble getting kids to do the Media Probe; they seem to enjoy it. But by the time people come to see me they have already made a decision to "do something" about television, so I may be seeing a unique population. Should your young adolescents seem unwilling to participate in the Media Probe, you might want to consider that time-honored tool of parenting, coercion. Say, for example, your kid wants to watch a program of questionable suitability, like "The Days and Nights of Molly Dodd," a fine program for adults, but one that deals with issues well beyond the world of the average thirteen-year-old. You might say, "OK, you can watch it once—but only if we run the Media Probe on it." I doubt you will need to use this strategy, since kids already play much more elaborate TV-based games on their own, but give it a whirl if needed.

Another thing to keep in mind is that the Media Probe is not restricted to the analysis of "stories." Since news programs, talk shows, and commercials all use a dramatic format and present issues and behaviors in conflict, the Media Probe can be used to investigate those programs as well—even MTV, but we will come to MTV in a moment.

As I implied above, the Media Probe is really a game, one you can play as a family or encourage your children to play with their friends. You can use it in adult discussion groups or at youth groups in your church or synagogue, although as your group gets older or more task- and values-oriented you may want to use the appendix version. You will discover that different people get very different messages from the same programs. You may discover that you have some serious fence mending to do with your children; or—more likely, if my workshops are any guide—you may discover that they have been listening and watching, and do share your values.

To summarize our developmental concerns issue for young adolescents then, we need to remember two important things. First, young adolescents have all the equipment they need to understand and interpret the world around them. What they lack is experience and, often, a clear understanding of their own values. Second, television provides an opportunity for you to work with your children, using the Media Probe, as you experience the wide variety of possible values and experiences represented by today's entertainment and information programs.

Sex and Violence

Parents of young adolescents are right to be concerned about the amount of sex and violence on television, particularly on the slick prime-time productions that are often the main staple of adolescent viewers. Again, we need to look back at the specific structure of television to realize why it offers so much sex and violence. Remember, television programs only exist to draw us to the commercials, so producers of television programs want to give us exactly what will draw us to the screen in large numbers. Sex, violence, and comedy draw people to the screen in large numbers. So we get programs with lots of sex, programs with lots of violence, programs with lots of laughter—and some programs that try with varying degrees of success to combine all three.

Also, and just as importantly, it is easy to write formula plots that focus on sex, or make people laugh, or seek solutions through violence. That is important because television is a voracious beast. It needs hundreds and thousands of hours of programming a week to keep it going. Say you have a basic cable system with no converter box—just 12 channels. Those channels run 24 hours a day, so 12 × 24 = 288 hours of programming a day; 288 × 7 = 2,016 hours of programming a week; 2,016 × 4 = 8,064 hours of programming a month; 8,064 × 12 = 96,768 hours of programming a year! I'll let you figure it out for a 30-channel system or a 60-channel system.

The point is that television demands lots of scripts. Scripts that focus on sex and violence are easy to write and attract the large numbers of viewers that generate the advertising revenues, that generate the profits, that pay the salaries, and pay the dividends, that support the owners who live in the house that sleaze built.

So what's a parent to do?

Reprinted by permission of NAS, Inc.

First, *control access*. Sounds familiar, doesn't it. Still even with young adolescents, you can control what they watch. Over the last couple of decades it has become increasingly in vogue to treat, and dress, ten- to fourteen-year-olds as though they were high school graduates. But they are children—older children, yes; children learning about growing up, yes; but still children. Treating them like adults does not make them adults. I am finding more and more college students in my classroom who stopped getting guidance from their parents when they were twelve or thirteen or fourteen. But they do not think like adults, they think like big twelve-, thirteen-, or fourteen-year-olds.

You still may well need to put some programs off limits that are overtly violent and sexual. Programs like "Miami Vice" and "The Avenger," even programs like "L.A. Law" and "St. Elsewhere," simply are not suitable for most young adolescents—even though young adolescents make up a sizable portion of the audience for those programs. A suggestion on strategy—do not make a big deal out of the viewing ban. Try saying something like, "Come on now, you know you don't watch that program."

"But I want to watch it."

"I can hear that you do."

"But ——— gets to watch it."

"I wish I could change it into a good program so you could watch it."

"Me too."

"Is there something else on you would like to watch?"

"No."

"Then let's turn off the tube for a while and ———." (See Chapter 6 to fill in the blank.)

Such an approach usually works a lot better than "Turn that program off this instant, you know you're not allowed to watch that!" Nothing makes a program more attractive than its ability to make a parent crazy.

Reprinted by permission of NAS, Inc.

The second way to handle your concern about sex and violence on TV is to use to your advantage the fact that adolescents do not watch much TV. If it has fallen into disuse, reactivate the viewing log. Remember the viewing log? That's where you and your children decide how many hours of television they can watch per day or per week, and then they select the programs in advance. This cuts down on the tendency to watch something sleazy because they just want to "watch TV" and that program happens to be on.

Third, keep a close eye on the PBS listings. The "Mystery" series and "Masterpiece Theatre" often run some programs suitable for young adolescents. And "Wonderworks" is the best consistent source for good adolescent programming around. Various PBS affiliates also occasionally pick up a show called "Degrassi Junior High," a wonderful program for—who else—junior high–aged kids, and those who aspire to that lofty station. You may have to lure your kids to these programs by initially offering them as a freebie: "OK, let's watch this show on "Wonderworks" together, I won't count it on your total this week." But they will soon be choosing it on their own, along with "Nova" and "Nature."

Fourth, make it a habit—or a requirement—to play the Media Probe with them on programs that you feel are introducing them to new or controversial issues that need discussing. Often programs with overt sexual or violent overtones provide excellent opportunities to discuss these issues with your children. Take the opportunity to clarify with them what the standards and expectations of the family are, and why.

Some Specific Thoughts on Sex and TV

Portrayals of sex on contemporary television, and the way young adolescents interpret those portrayals, perpetuate some sexual myths that can be dangerous and downright life-threatening in the eighties. First, people don't get pregnant. Consider J. R. on Dallas, for example. He has hopped in and out of more beds than you can count with only one "accident." And J. R. is not alone. Most daytime and night-time soap operas are filled with casual cohabitation resulting in an astonishingly low pregnancy rate.

Second, people don't use birth control on TV, or at least they don't talk about it. I was reading the *Proceedings* from the July 1988 Medical/Science Writers' Conference sponsored by the American Academy of Pediatrics, and I came across some interesting statistics in this area. The *Proceedings* report that, according to a Harris poll, American children view an average of over 14,000 sexual references and innuendoes on television each year. Of these, less than 150 refer to the use of birth control. This rate of unprotected sex makes the dearth of pregnancies on television even more unlikely—but it is amazing how things work out when results are determined by script writers and not biology.

Third, only people in miniseries or made-for-TV movies get AIDS. Other sexually transmitted diseases seem to be almost nonexistent, although condoms are rarely mentioned.

Fourth, "making love," that phrase that we grew up with in the sixties to express physical intimacy and our preference for it to making war, has been replaced by "having sex." This linguistic phenomenon seems apparent both on television and in real life, and I worry about the perception of sex it seems to reflect. Television's depiction of sex seems to hover around extreme and unenviable poles. On one hand you have the model of sexual involvement found on shows like "Dynasty" or "Dallas": sex is cold, manipulative, exploitive. On the other hand you have the daytime soap opera version in which sex is tempestuous, passionate, and uncontrollable. Neither depiction strikes me as healthy or desirable.

A final myth projected by television is that beautiful, sexy people are sexually active. There are a lot of hidden barbs in this myth. First of all, there is the issue of attractiveness. Let's face it—there aren't many plain people on television. Even local TV news anchors and weatherpeople tend to look more like models than the boy or girl next door. Television stars tend to be beautiful—in a very traditional, mainstream, *Cosmopolitan* and *Gentleman's Quarterly* kind of way. Second, these television people—at least in the TV dramas—tend to be sexually active. The double message to young adolescents is that they ought to be beautiful or handsome; but if they cannot manage that, at least they should be sexually active and salvage some little bit of popular respectability. The absurdity of that message would be funny if kid's didn't take it dead seriously. And they do take it seriously. Just look at the clothes and makeup on today's junior high school kids. Just talk to my wife, Susan, a health educator who does workshops on adolescent sexuality with elementary, junior high, and high school students. The level of sexual interest and activity of the children she works with is enough to curl the hair of even the most liberal old hippy.

These myths—or perceptions, if you prefer—are by-products of television today and should be addressed in our media probe discussions of sex and television. However, if you are—like many of us are— a little leery of discussing these topics with your young adolescents, let me suggest a couple of books by experts in the field that you might find helpful: *Raising a Child Conservatively in a Sexually Permissive World*, by Sol Gordon and Judith Gordon (New York: Simon and Schuster, 1983). Yes, again. It really is an excellent book. *The Sexual Adolescent: Communicating with Teen-agers about Sex*, by Sol Gordon, Peter Scales, and Kathleen Everly (Boston: Duxbury Press, 1979) is a more "scholarly" book but has lots of good references and information.

I also suggest that you consult with your minister, rabbi, school guidance counselor, etc., for other resources that might be available in your community. Our children do not live in a world where "no information is better than misinformation." Sadly, we live in a time when either could kill them.

Some Specific Thoughts on Violence and TV

Scholars have been researching the question of the impact of television violence for a number of years. One of their primary concerns has been the effect of television violence on children. And while no one study has demonstrated an incontestable correlation between watching television violence and behaving violently, the weight of that body of literature has led me to some of the following beliefs and concerns. First, while television no longer blindly argues that "might *makes* right," it certainly argues that if you *are* right then it is quite acceptable to use might—sometimes excessive might—to enforce your "right-

ness." Second, force and violence on television are purely physical issues. Being in a fight seems to leave no emotional scars, no lingering mental discomfort—unless it is a determination to be the "winner" next time.

I have trouble with both these common characteristics of televised violence. They are obvious fictions. The first is a legal fiction—as any law enforcement officer will tell you. If someone decides to take an unauthorized swim in your pool or walk on your lawn, it is *not* safe to assume that you may punctuate your request that he or she leave with the firearm of your choice. The second is a psychological fiction, as any mental health professional will attest. We have thousands of Vietnam veterans walking around with posttraumatic delayed stress syndrome, tragic evidence of the psychic toll violence extracts from soldiers—regardless of who "wins" the fight. Yet both these fictions are presented as truth in many action/crime/adventure programs—as well as in almost all televised National Hockey League games. They are dangerous fictions that—if unchallenged by the attentive and concerned parent—can lead our children into physically and psychologically dangerous behaviors.

Violence is therefore an area that you will want to pay particular attention to with your children. Again, the Media Probe can be helpful in isolating those situations in the various dramas where violence is used, and in getting a discussion started about if, or under what circumstances, violence is an appropriate behavior.

Some Specific Thoughts on Music Videos

Music videos first came floating down television's electronic river in 1981 on the nation's first all-music video channel, MTV. In the beginning MTV went into only 2 million cable households, but that really did not bother its originators, because the network was not seen as a money maker in its own right. Rather, the idea was that the videos—mostly by young, relatively unknown groups—would serve as commercials for those groups, increasing sales and raising profits in the recording industry.

Well, so much for planning. MTV became the exception to the industry rule that teenagers do not watch TV. Kids began to watch four, five, even six hours of MTV a week, and the industry—never one to miss the opportunity to make another buck—realized that they could, given the audience they were attracting, charge advertisers good money to show *their* commercials in between MTV's own commercials—the videos. Sort of a commercial sandwich.

The rest is history, as folks are fond of saying. MTV is now delivered, according to their research department, into 43 million cable homes, and it competes with several copycat cable programs, some broadcast competition, and its own spin-off, VH-1.

All this success has had an effect on the programming. Initially the videos were commercials for the bands, and as a result were fairly representative of how the bands visualized their music, because the intent was to get viewers to purchase the compact disc, the record, the tape, or the concert ticket. Now, however, the videos have become the "program." Since, as on any other commercial network, the function of the program is to draw viewers to the commercials, MTV gives viewers what they want to see, not necessarily what the bands feel is the best way to visualize their music. As a result there has been a great deal of cross-pollination between music videos and regular prime-time entertainment programs. "Miami Vice" is often one long music video, and many music videos are miniature soap operas.

Music videos have not been at all shy about borrowing from commercial programming the elements sure to draw large audiences: sex and violence. But, despite the bad press music videos often receive, there is no firm evidence that music videos are—categorically—sexier or more violent than normal prime-time fare.

Of course that certainly does not mean that music videos should pass unfettered into your child's television lineup. I have not seen many videos on MTV, VH-1, Nighttracks, Video Soul, etc., that I would be wild about having my kids watch much before high school. On the other hand, music videos are a form of programming that kids are getting a great deal of exposure to, if not at home then at friends' homes—particularly those with older brothers and sisters. In light of this, it becomes really important to sit down with your children and watch the music videos that they want to watch. You should still use the Media Probe and pay particular attention to how music videos treat the relationship between children and adults, the way they portray women and minorities, and the basic values that seem to underlie the behaviors that the various videos seem to advocate.

You will find, as you find on regular television, a lot of self-centered, violent, sexy, shallow material. However, many are surprised to discover that there are some really good music videos out there. Music and television are a natural fit—and when done right can be quite enjoyable, beautiful, and even moving. You need to sit down with your children and learn together which videos fit in which categories.

Finally, it is worthwhile to note that the music video form is being drawn into the area of children's television with some success. "Kidsongs" is a syndicated series of children's music videos that is shown over a number of local stations; "Babysongs," which I discuss in the last chapter, is available in an appealing tape of music videos for the very young.

Commercials

If you remember our discussion about young children and commercials, our major concern in this area was to teach them the Golden Rule of Television Number Three: *Commercials* are different from *programs*. But then we ran into program-length commercials, whole programs that try to sell you a product, whether it be a My Little Pony Castle or a Captain Power Spacecraft. We have to confront a similar problem as we examine the potential impact of commercials upon young adolescents.

To begin with, we need to amend the third rule to read: *Commercials* are different from *real life*. We need to make this rule as clear as we can because of the interaction between three related issues.

The first issue is the parade of possibilities that television offers to adolescents. As we discussed at the beginning of the chapter, adolescents do not see television as completely true or completely false; when they watch "Cosby" or "Different World," or "Family Ties," or "Growing Pains"—all programs that feature young adolescents making decisions about life—they realize they are watching fiction, but they also realize that they are watching *possible* ways in which to behave.

Second is the issue of *parasocial relationships*. A strange term—for me it always calls up the image of a couple dancing a fox-trot in combat fatigues. But it actually means an imaginary relationship that exists between an audience member and a media performer. The idea was first discussed by psychiatrists in the 1950s and has gained considerable credibility as the world of the media has continued to evolve.

As an example, let's use the obvious cases—talk-show hosts. We can choose Carson or Letterman or, to a lesser extent, Winfrey or Donahue—any host whose relationship to the viewer *appears* to be personal. Carson is perhaps the best at carrying off this pseudo-personal relationship. He manifests all the appropriate behaviors of a good friend: he maintains eye contact with us, his witty asides always include us as co-conspirators, he is a funny conversationalist, he brings interesting and famous guests with him into our living rooms and bedrooms, and he never spills his drink on the couch or leaves cigarette burns on the carpets. Who could ask for a nicer friend? So we visit with him night after night; we tolerate his vacations, his guest hosts, and his divorces because he is always so nice to us, so much fun to have around. Furthermore, we get a little upset upon finding ourselves in a hotel room either without a TV—perish the thought—or equipped with one that does not give us the station with Johnny. We miss our friend.

If we, as reasonably well-adjusted adults, can strike up this kind of relationship with a television character, is it any surprise that young adolescents—anxious to try on all the faces of their futures—might take the process one step further? And on occasion they do. Sometimes the heroes of television blend a bit into the world of everyday reality. Most of the results of this reality warp are relatively harmless, affecting primarily language and dress, although sometimes more serious behavioral symptoms emerge.

The third issue is the submerged-product commercial that submerges the product in a *lifestyle* that the advertiser wants us to associate with the product. Michelob beer has run several campaigns of this type. Both the "Night belongs to Michelob" and the "You can have it all" campaigns are filled with highly stylized images of beautiful, young affluent people doing fun and exciting things in attractive settings. Nothing is said about the beer itself; there is no mention of the quality of the grain, the water, or the expertise of the master brewer, none of that product-specific information we used to hear about beer. All we see are exquisitely produced images of the lifestyle of which the beer—the advertiser hopes we will conclude—is an integral part. All we hear is upbeat contemporary music that—again the advertiser hopes—sounds like the soundtrack we would choose for our own lives.

Levi's does the same thing with its 501 jeans commercials. Again, they provide no comment on the characteristics of the product; instead MTV-style images and music convey an aura of youth, attractiveness, and "hipness," with that ever-paradoxical adolescent blend of aloofness and vulnerability. The jeans could be made from recycled

Reprinted by permission of NAS, Inc.

newsprint for all the ad company cares; what is important is the image the commercials construct for the product.

Now, how do these three issues—television as a parade of possibilities, parasocial relationships, and submerged-product lifestyle commercials—shape the relationship between young adolescents and commercials? We can clearly see how they are connected in a recent set of Pepsi commercials featuring Michael J. Fox, the young star of "Family Ties." As we examine the commercials we need to remember that Fox, young, attractive, and talented, is quite likely the media half of millions of parasocial relationships with young adolescents. In these commercials Fox demonstrates how it is possible to impress girls by being reckless and carefree in a video montage that has nothing to do with the specific qualities of the product being advertised. For parents, these kinds of commercials—and there are lots of them—raise a number of concerns.

First, and most significantly, the message implies strongly that there is a vital link between the things you possess and your value as a person. Elementary school and junior high school students do not clamor for certain labels on their jeans or sunglasses because their parents have told them they should—at least I certainly hope not. More likely their media "friends" have been paid huge sums of money to tell them, or at least strongly imply, that in order to be part of their particular "lifestyle" they need to eat, dress in, wash with, smear on, or smell like the advertised products. The bottom line? You are what you buy.

And that brings us to our second concern—buying things. When we talk with younger children about commercials, a couple of our best arguments are "You don't really need that," and "Do you really want to spend your money on that?" Those arguments often work because there is no real sense of urgency to possess the product being advertised. At other times the best way to handle preadolescent advertising-induced needs is to suggest a game of catch or a visit to the park.

Such approaches are no longer effective with the kinds of advertisements we are discussing here. The psychological manipulation that goes on with these ads plays on the young adolescent's normal feelings of insecurity and uncertainty, on their strong need to be liked and accepted by their peers. As a result the urgency these young adolescents feel to possess the "things" in question is significant. This need can be resolved in a number of unsatisfactory ways: (1) you buy the product—creating a never-ending cycle of acquisition and expense that confirms the link between material possessions and self-worth; (2) you make the young person get a job or do odd jobs around the house in order to earn the item desired—and in doing so teach the child that work is merely a route to the possession of goods and has no inherent value, challenge, or enjoyment in its own right; or (3) you refuse to purchase the item, condemning your child—in his or her eyes anyhow—to life as a social outcast.

A more satisfactory alternative is to go back to the third golden rule of television (amended): Commercials are different from real life. From this starting point you can sit down and talk to your children about the reality of how goods are bought and sold and how young people get conned into spending a lot of money on junk. You make it clear that you are not going to spend your hard-earned money on junk, but give them the freedom to spend their money if they choose —with the following stipulation: they have to research the market. If they want to buy a particular brand of something, they need to define a list of criteria for judging the quality of what they want to buy. For clothes—in addition to the inevitable demands of "style"—durability and ease of care become important. Flexibility—how often and in what situations an article of clothing can be worn—also becomes an issue. Cost is always important—is one of brand X preferable to the three of brand Y you could buy for the same money?

Reality demands some comments on this approach. It certainly is not foolproof. Even after doing their research they may decide that the best product *is* the one that Michael Fox or Michael Jackson is pushing. But at least they will have thought about the process, and in thinking about the process they begin to acquire the skills of reasonable consumption, of wise shopping. Also, you need to decide when to invoke the market research requirement; if the difference between brands of soft drinks seems negligible, I would let that one slide. However, when your eleven-year-old announces that just "everyone" is wearing Guess jeans to T-ball practice, it is time to break out the old market research gambit. You might even want to mention the trade deficit. Finally, you need to realize that you are not making your kids social lepers by refusing to knuckle under to the latest Madison Avenue consumer coup. As a matter of fact, the kid who can provide six good reasons for not doing what everybody else is doing might well become one of the class opinion leaders.

Finally, you can go out and collect all the commercials you can find for the product—video, radio, print, billboards, whatever—and subject them all to the Media Probe with your kid. Examine the behaviors in the ads, figure out what the values are, try to see what values motivate what behaviors—and then decide what all that has to do with the product being advertised. It is often an eye-opening experience for the adolescent to see the ends that people will go to in order to get us to buy something. As with the market research approach, they still may want the product—but in a less frenzied, more rational way. Furthermore, many times the child will get turned off by the whole process and refuse to have anything to do with the product.

I can hear it now . . . , "No, Daddy, get those Calvin Kleins out of here, I'll pick up something off the bargain rack at K-Mart." Well, it *could* happen, maybe. Seriously, the effect may not be that extreme, but it is a helpful process and a good experience for both the parent and the child.

Looking back on it I realize that this chapter may seem pretty directive, but we need to remember that direction is what most young adolescents are looking for at this point in their lives. It is a confusing time, with new feelings, new frustrations, and changing bodies. A little guidance is a welcome, but rarely asked for, commodity. Television gives advice without being asked, but it is a river full of electronic sand banks, this television river of ours. It is peopled with video versions of painted ladies and cardsharps. But, like Tom and Huck's Mississippi, it also holds some pleasant sheltered places, some places of rare beauty. If we become the pilots, guiding our children past the rough spots, we can help them find some valuable friends along its banks, as long as we remember to watch our step and hold fast to the Media Probe.

5

You and Me against the World: Confronting TV's Technology and the Industry

We moved not too long ago. We have survived for the most part; the sea of cardboard boxes has drifted out with the weekly tide of trash pickups, or the boxes have been broken down and passed on to others on the packing side of moving.

The hard part of moving—at least for us—is reestablishing the basic survival systems. The kitchen is a dominant concern. In the new house we have more cupboard space, but less drawer space. What goes where? The sink and the range are now across from each other instead of next to each other—where do the support utensils for each belong?

I suppose it has always been that way. Hauling the treasured old chest of drawers out of the Conestoga, the battered family trunk out of steerage, the icebox off the flatbed of a '38 Ford are just different choruses in the same American folk song. But I have spent the last few days singing a little ditty few of my forebears had to deal with. It goes something like this:

> Well, I'm lying on the floor,
> The baby's sittin' on my head.
> Old coaxial cable's
> Knotted up like sewin' thread
> I've got those low-down
> Hookin' up the TV blues.
>
> Well, the vcr won't play back.
> The remote control is gone.
> The converter box got dropped
> Somewhere out there on the lawn

I've got those low-down
Hookin' up the TV blues.

You may well ask why I go through it all. As a matter of fact I asked myself that question several times over the last few days, once while waiting—on hold—to make an appointment to have the cable hooked up, once while driving to the cable company's office to replace a faulty remote, once while trying to duplicate the wiring and switching system necessary to watch one program while recording another, and once again while trying to figure out why I could get sound but no picture from the vcr. I remembered why I go through it every time I turned on the "uncabled" TV up in the bedroom: I do it because otherwise I am trapped by the offerings of my local TV broadcast stations.

There was a time when television *was* broadcast programs. In each town you could get few stations, more when the weather was one way, fewer when it was another. But, as we noted in Chapter 1, television can now offer a video bookstore of seemingly infinite variety. That variety is largely the result of two technological innovations: cable television and video cassette recorders (vcrs). Together they have changed the world of television and they have paradoxically given us, the viewers, more power than we have ever had to control and influence the video messages we choose to allow into our homes. In this chapter we will examine two notions: taming the technology by making television's new gadgets work *for* us and making the viewer's voice heard, with an eye toward maximizing our impact upon the producers of video programming. Let's look at the technology first.

Video Cassette Recorders

In mid-1988 Roger D. Percy, the people-meter man, estimated that there were vcrs in 50 percent of America's households (*Christian Science Monitor*, April 20, 1988, p. 24). Far from being frivolous toys, the vcr is one of the most liberating bits of technology to come along since the typewriter and the mimeograph machine. I think most of us buy vcrs because of the freedom they give us to choose what we want to watch, when we want to watch it, and how we want to watch it. That is no small victory. Before discussing how to acquire a vcr without selling the farm, let's look at each of these new freedoms individually.

Choosing What We Want to Watch

From the beginning of television until the advent of the vcr, we had to watch what was being broadcast at the time or watch nothing. The

VCR allows us to accumulate a library of tapes so that we can watch whatever we want. There are two ways to go about accumulating this library: taping off the air and purchasing prerecorded tapes. And in addition to creating your own library, you can find tapes at the public library and the various video rental outlets.

Ever since the Philips company began to market its N1500 back in 1972, people have been recording programs off the air to keep and view at their discretion. However, it wasn't until 1984 that everyone agreed it was legal. That was the year that the Supreme Court ruled, in consideration of a suit brought against Sony by MCA Inc. and Walt Disney Productions, that home taping of broadcast programming is not a violation of copyright laws. Across the country people heaved huge sighs of relief to realize they had not been doing wrong all those years, and there was no need now to stuff those "Andy Griffith Show" tapes down the toilet before the video police came knocking at their doors.

I am not going to tell you how to run your VCR. That is what the instruction booklets are for, and most of them can actually be understood these days. What I want to talk about in this section is how to get from the *idea* of wanting to tape something for your library to the *actuality* of having that program on a tape in a usable form. Those of you who have eighty-four hours of unviewed, unlabeled tapes stuffed in a cabinet somewhere know that this is not as easy as it sounds.

Like viewing programs, taping programs becomes easier and more successful if planned in advance. What you need to do is sit down with your kids and go through the *TV Guide* or weekly listings. As you mark the programs they wish to watch in their viewing log, you can also jot down any programs you might want to tape. There are a number of good reasons for doing this, but primarily it saves you from realizing that you want to tape a program fifteen seconds before it airs. In that situation you usually dive frantically for the tape repository looking for a tape to use, grab whatever you can find, and end up taping "Miss Piggy Goes to Law School" over the only existing uncolorized copy of *Casablanca* left in your state. You need to set up a taping schedule so that you can get a properly cued and labeled tape into the machine before panic sets in.

Once you have your schedule, you also need to figure out some way to remember it. The VCR makers have attempted to help us out in this area by giving us fourteen-day, fourteen-event programmable VCRs. You can program these machines to tape fourteen events over a two-week period. Then, assuming there is enough tape in the machine, the VCR will blithely turn off and on and even change channels until it has done your electronic bidding. I do not know any people who have actually done this successfully, but the machines are fully capable of doing it.

I suggest a different method using paper and scotch tape:

1. Make up your taping schedule. Cover about a week at a time, and try to hold the line at about three programs a week. Write each program down with big magic marker letters (good practice for the kiddies!) on its own sheet of paper. We use this kind of form:

> Monday, 7 P.M., Channel 4
> Anne of Green Gables
> 2 Hours

2. Tape these sheets in highly visible, often-used areas. We use the refrigerator door, although when that gets too full of messages to notice any new ones, we move the show sheets to the door of the cupboard that holds the coffee cups.

3. On the day of the program, or a day or so before if you really do not want to miss the show, tape the show sheet to the TV.

4. Read the sheet, get the appropriate tape, revise the label by adding the show you are about to tape, and insert the tape in the VCR. Check the tape to make sure you are where you want to be on the tape, not recording over another program you wish to save or leaving long gaps of blanks between programs.

5. Prepare the machine for taping. Here is where you need to decide whether to use the programmable feature of the VCR or the "Super Extended Play" safety method. The programmable method simply entails programming your VCR to turn on and tape the program in question, shutting itself off when it is done. Whether this is really simple or not depends upon your particular VCR.

The "Super Extended Play" safety method entails setting your VCR on its longest play setting (usually a four- or six-hour option). You then manually start the tape so that the program you wish to tape will be "caught" somewhere on those four or six hours of taping. This usually results in your getting three or four or five hours of programs you do not want—but it is an almost foolproof way to get that show you just have to have. I also need to point out that on some machines picture and sound quality drop off significantly in the extended play modes, so the "Super Extended Play" safety method is a questionable taping strategy for concerts and other programs where video and audio quality is of great importance.

These steps may seem a primitive way of controlling such high-tech machines, but the use of paper and scotch tape, or derivations thereof, seem to be quite common and effective in VCR households—especially those with small children. Kids, it seems, have an uncanny ability to eradicate all instructions you have given a fourteen-day, fourteen-event VCR with one well-placed bump of an elbow.

Whatever your system for reminding yourself to get the program on tape, you also need to implement some system of tape labeling or you will go absolutely crazy trying to keep track of your tapes. Although you will want to devise the system that will work best for you, I do have a couple of suggestions.

First, set aside individual tapes for programs you collect regularly. For example, when Andrea was just starting preschool, a lovely children's program, "Today's Special," was airing—on the Nickelodeon Channel, I believe—between 8:30 and 9:00 A.M. Well, Andrea had to leave for school at about 8:45, so she could never see all of "Today's Special." We quickly decided not even to begin watching the program in the morning, but rather to record the program for her to watch in the afternoon. So we set aside a tape marked "Today's Special" and taped the program every morning. That way—on extended play—we could get twelve episodes of the program on each tape, and we would always know what tape the programs were on. We did the same with other programs that we wanted to have in our library—"Sesame Street," "Mister Rogers' Neighborhood," etc., initially and, later, programs like "Nature" and "National Geographic Special," which she enjoyed, but which came on after her bedtime. Now those tapes are still easily identifiable for passing along to her little sister.

Second, occasionally go through your tapes and reevaluate those marked "Sports Events" and "Keep this tape!" You will undoubtedly discover that you have a goodly number of hours of tape devoted to things you are not really sure you want to keep, and you may even wonder why you taped them in the first place. This situation prompts a sort of video spring cleaning—nasty, but necessary.

Third, and this is a warning made necessary by the proliferation of camcorders, VHS movie systems, and all those other home video systems with cameras that are sweeping the country. Store those home tapes—your baby's first steps, birthday parties, graduations, confirmations, baptisms, and Bar Mitzvahs—in an entirely different place from your off-the-air recordings. You want to make absolutely sure not to record over them by accident. "Anne of Green Gables" will always be available somewhere, but your baby's first steps never come around in summer reruns for you to tape again. To protect these and other tapes from being accidentally erased or taped over, learn the location of and remove the record protect tab on your videocassettes. On a typical VHS tape it is located on the front edge, near the label.

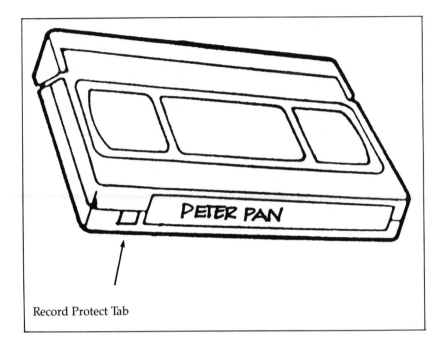

Record Protect Tab

Purchasing Prerecorded Tapes. It is in the area of prerecorded tapes that television shows its new face. When I first began to pay attention to children's videotapes seven or eight years ago, the commercial home use market was almost nonexistent. Today, I am sure I will neglect reviewing some fine children's tapes for you in the book's final chapter because the companies producing them will come into existence after we go to press. It is a mushrooming industry—with some exquisite offerings, some musty fungus, and some poisonous toadstools.

Since the final chapter of the book attempts to distinguish between the good, the bad, and the ugly in the area of family video fare, in this section I will stick to the *process* of deciding what videotapes to purchase. This becomes an important question because, although purchase prices are coming down, most bargain videos are still priced significantly above comparable hardcover children's books.

A few simple rules will keep us from making expensive mistakes. The first rule is, *do not buy anything you have not seen.* I don't care how attractive the sales literature is, or how many stars or experts recommend it. It is your money: make sure the product meets your specifications and is compatible with your values. The only exceptions to this rule are those instances in which you have the option to return the tape and get your money back; however, such options are rare and understandably so, as they force the producer/distributor into a very vulnerable position. So if you are not going to buy anything before you see it, how are you going to see it before you buy it? Well, that is a very good question for which I have some partial answers.

Libraries seem to be of at least two minds about children's videotapes. I have been to some libraries that carry delightful video collections, and the librarians talk animatedly about using videotapes to draw children into the world of literature. I have also talked with librarians who are openly antagonistic to *anything* on television, apparently believing that all children's television is a mindless rip-off. Usually, however, financial reasons keep libraries from providing children's videos. The director of my public library estimates that it would cost between a quarter- and a half-million dollars to start a quality video program for our library system. An effort restricted purely to children's video would not be nearly that costly, but it would still be a considerable expenditure. In any case, if your public library does have a collection of children's videos, it is often an excellent place to find items you want to review before purchasing them for your home library.

Another source of tapes might be your child's school. Schools are becoming more and more involved in the use of video to augment traditional programs in literature, science, language, and fine arts, and they often allow parents to review their tapes. You can also ask around the neighborhood, or at your place of worship, or at PTA. When kids or their parents come across a good tape they are quite willing to talk about it, and they might even be willing to loan it for preview, perhaps in exchange for one of yours. They might also be able to tell you about tapes that are not worth your time and energy.

I mentioned earlier that very few companies have a return policy. But some of them will send you preview tapes with some excerpts from their catalog. While this is a poor second to actually being able to see the entire tape, it is quite preferable to buying blind. The newer companies specializing in children's videos are much more likely to have this service.

The second rule is, *Look for tapes your children will enjoy watching many times.* Try not to waste your money on tapes *you* want them to watch, but instead get them quality tapes *they* will want to go back to time and again. It is a fine line to tread. Let me give you an example. I might want my kids to watch Masterpiece Theatre's version of "Pride and Prejudice," but they have only given it cursory attention in a review session. It is a bad purchase risk. On the other hand, say they love *Pee-Wee's Big Adventure*, but I find it problematic for six-year-olds. Purchase of that tape defeats the purpose of a home library. Finally we come to *Lady and the Tramp*. It is not great literature, but it is a delightful video and the kids love it. That's a good purchase option. Now you shop around for the best price.

The third rule is, *Do not buy anything you can tape off the air for free.* That seems to be obvious, as are the exceptions—special purchases for summer vacations, sick kids, etc.

Renting Tapes. People use their VCRs primarily to play rented tapes. The children's portion of the rental industry must not be very profitable, though; for the most part selections are limited, featuring mostly the program-length commercials we talked about in Chapter 3. However, a couple of areas in particular are worth investigating.

Most rental outlets carry most of the old Disney classics, some *Winnie the Pooh*, an occasional *Wind in the Willows*. Rental is a good way to see if these tapes have enough repeat appeal or content quality to warrant a purchase. And I do strongly recommend that you preview even your old childhood favorites—memory can play strange tricks on us, and what we remember as a classic may only have been an above-average tape from what was, after all, a very limited children's movie market. So view it again and then make your decision about purchase.

Recalling our discussions about the appeal of music and dance in Chapters 2 and 3, you can also find some real jewels on the more neglected racks of your neighborhood videotape rental outlet. My older girl fell in love with *Gigi* when she was about three and has maintained a strong affinity for the likes of *The Music Man*, *My Fair Lady*, and, interestingly, *Calamity Jane* well into her seventh year. The baby hoots and claps along with many of the musical numbers, although I must confess her attention wanders shamefully during the longer stretches of dialogue. In any case, check out the musicals section; it is sometimes a double bargain since many of the films you find there can be bought for relatively low prices through discount stores and catalogs like *Publisher's Clearinghouse*. Finally, a quick word of warning. A lot of these musicals were produced in the thirties, forties, and fifties. They are for the most part blatantly sexist, and when minorities appear at all, the roles are stereotypical. Finding positive minority role models remains difficult in current offerings as well. BET (Black Entertainment Television) and SIN (Spanish International Network) fill some adult needs but offer little for kids. So preview closely and be prepared to correct those perceptions.

Choosing When We Want to Watch

Television affects our daily schedule in a number of subtle and not-so-subtle ways. The morning news gently nudges shower schedules

and breakfast timing. I mentioned earlier that morning programming for children was causing us some logistical problems in making the preschool carpool. "Sesame Street" and "Mister Rogers' Neighborhood" are delightfully scheduled for winding the kids down before dinner—if you happen to eat dinner at around 5:30, no easy task for working couples or those on schedules other than 9 to 5. The evening news has a way of inviting itself to the dinner table, often with terrible taste and questionable manners.

The VCR allows you to choose not only your own programs, as we discussed above, but also your own schedules. Back in Chapter 3 we discussed the problem of the overt and conceptually disjointed violence that is often a feature of the evening news. I argued that we ought not to expose small children to that type of programming. The VCR allows you to tape the news so that you can watch it after the children are in bed.

An additional benefit to choosing your own schedules is that you do not feel nearly as tied to the TV as you might without a VCR. The need to stay in touch with the tube in case you "miss something" diminishes. A whole new dimension opens up in the television debates. Remember playing this scene with your kids?

> You: Turn off the TV and come on up to dinner.
> LOYL (Light of your life): It's almost over, I'll be there in a minute.
> You: [Noting that it is seven minutes after the hour] It is not almost over, turn it off and come up here.
> LOYL: But I really want to see this.
> You: That show isn't on your viewing log and dinner is on the table come on!!
> LOYL: You never let me watch what I want!
> You: If I have to come down there, you are in big trouble young lady!

And it goes downhill from there. Now picture that same scene with a VCR.

> You: Turn off the TV and come on up to dinner.
> LOYL: It's almost over, I'll be there in a minute.
> You: [Noting that it is seven minutes after the hour] It is not almost over, turn it off and come up here.
> LOYL: But I really want to see this.
> You: Toss a tape in and record it. Dinner's getting cold. You can watch that later.
> LOYL: OK.

Now, isn't that better? And the best thing about it is that 70 percent of the time they never go back and watch the rest of the program, so you have begun to break the ties to the TV.

The scheduling freedom you gain also allows you to use television to smooth over some rough spots. For example, the babysitter transition scene—when the babysitter arrives and you try to leave. Suddenly separation anxiety wells up in a child who has managed to drive you crazy all day. She gets a death grip on your knee and begins to howl.

In this situation the VCR can help out a great deal. First, you set up one of your child's favorite tapes to overlap the babysitter's arrival time and your departure time. Then when the sitter arrives, you put the tape on pause, and say something like this:

> You: Come give us a kiss and say goodnight, honey. Oh, I don't think Michele has seen this tape. When we leave why don't you tell her what's happened so far, and you can watch the rest together. Then hop to bed, OK?
> LOYL: OK. G'nite, Mom, G'nite, Dad. Well, Michele, Rikki-Tikki-Tavi is a mongoose. Mongooses kill snakes, and there's this cobra named Nag and . . . (Mom and Dad exit stage right, laughing all the way!)

Admittedly, being able to "time shift" your television viewing schedule is not going to solve all your family squabbles, but it does give tranquillity and accord a powerful new ally.

Choosing How We Want to Watch

"How" we watch is dependent on our relationship to our old friend the commercial. On a broadcast program there is little we can do about the time that commercials occupy. We have become quite adept at filling that time. I often tell my students that one of the greatest gifts America has given to the rest of the industrialized world is the ability to cook a four-course meal, read a magazine, *and* go to the bathroom during a single commercial break. vcrs, especially those with remote control, threaten that cultural adaptation.

We can now affect the time that commercials spend on our screens. As long as we have a program on tape, we can speed right through the commercials by simply hitting the fast-forward button. It is called "zipping" by folks in the industry. Advertisers, understandably, do not like zipping at all and are trying to find ways of blunting its impact. One idea I have heard is that we will begin to see a product name or logo on the screen, in the same spot, throughout the entire commercial. The effect is that even when you "zip" the commercial the product name or logo will remain legible. I guess their reasoning is that it is better than nothing.

If you prefer "nothing," especially in programs that you want to collect for your home library, you can do what I do for my mother. If everyone were like my mother, the networks would have crumbled long ago: since she cannot stand commercials, my mother only watches pbs. Being a media critic by trade I am uncomfortable with the idea that Mom is missing *everything* on commercial television, because it has some good things to offer. So every once in a while, I sit down and tape a few of my favorites for her, carefully hitting the pause button during all the commercials so that the final product is a tape of the program that is entirely free of commercials. This strategy ("zapping") is particularly beneficial when I am collecting decent children's programming that, in its natural state, is surrounded by commercials for refined sugar and plastic in an infinite variety of forms. By editing out the commercials I can create good programming and eliminate offensive messages.

Another new wrinkle on how we watch TV that a vcr provides is "viewer controlled continuity." Again, with a broadcast program scene follows scene at the broadcast pace. If the phone rings, if dinner is ready, if bedtime strikes, a regularly broadcast program grinds blindly on, uncontrollable. With a vcr we have the same control over video that we have over books. We can "pick it up" when we want to and "put it down" at will.

The vcr also allows us to rewind and review scenes (as well as "zip" through others); in short, we control the pace of the program.

This element of pace is important when we watch programs with the kids. On one level it allows us to repeat elements of the program that they may not have understood on first viewing. "There, did you see how Mr. Wizard did that? No? OK, let's rewind and take another look."

On another level pace also helps us teach the three golden rules of television. "No, honey. This is a commercial. Let's back up a bit. See how the screen goes black? That means a commercial is coming. Now look at this picture. Can you see anybody from your show? No? That's because this is a commercial. What do you think they want us to buy?"

On a final level, and one that is related to all the uses of a VCR, controlling the pace of the programs demystifies television. It makes the images less real. If a child knows that she controls what characters "come to life" on her TV, if she knows that she can turn them off, make them go backwards or forwards or stand still, then she comes to understand—at a very basic and important level—that television is *not* reality. She realizes that Mom and Dad are real, that her brothers and sisters are real, that school and friends are real, but that television is only television.

Shopping for a VCR

I have no intention of talking brand names with you. Frankly, I do not think they matter much. But there are some factors you need to consider before you rush out to purchase one of these marvelous machines. As I implied earlier, they are now making VCRs with more bells and whistles than the space shuttle. You really do not need most of them, but some of them are vital to getting the most out of your machine.

Programmable Timers. All VCRs have a timer that lets you record a program while you are out dining with the kids at Chez McDonalds. The fourteen-day, fourteen-event model was advertised for $199.95 just the other day. I have had VCRs of various shapes and designs in my home for eleven or twelve years now, and only once have I set my VCR to record something as much as forty-eight hours ahead. That once was when we were leaving home on Friday and were not going to get back in time to tape a Sunday afternoon special. Other than that one time, simply being able to program twenty-four hours in advance has been quite sufficient. They do not make "twenty-four-hour only" VCRs, but if you can save some money by going to a seven-day, four-event programmable option, do it.

Video Heads. You will see machines advertised as having two, three, or four heads. Heads are the elements in the machine that actually touch the tape, either to lay down the magnetic signals for the sound and picture (record), or to pick up and reproduce those signals (playback). The number of heads usually correlates quite closely to picture quality—the more heads, the better the picture, because as the number of heads increases, the job each head is asked to do decreases. More importantly, the number of heads and the quality of the picture critically affect the function of on-screen search, which allows you to see the picture as you fast-forward or rewind the tape to find a particular image. On-screen search is a vital feature, since otherwise you literally have to run the machine blind. If your machine does not have on-screen search, or if it works poorly, you will not only have a very difficult time finding out where you are on any particular tape, you also won't be able to zip through commercials.

As I have already said, the quality of on-screen search is usually related to the number of recording or playback heads there are on the VCR. However, video technology is a rapidly changing technology, and new heads might quickly void this statement. In fact, when our old and venerable VCR finally died recently, I found an inexpensive two-head machine to replace it that has quite acceptable on-screen search picture quality. Remember that you do not want to watch the tape on on-screen search; you just need to find out where you are. To be sure that you are getting the on-screen search quality you need, take a tape with you when you go VCR shopping. The tape should be recorded at the slowest speed, the six-hour mode for a two-hour tape (T-120). When you are seriously considering buying a machine, pop that tape in and run it back and forth a few times in the on-screen search mode. If you cannot see the picture easily and clearly, shop on—that machine is not for you.

Recording speed. Another fatal flaw in a machine is the lack of an extended play (EP) mode, which will record and play six hours of programming on a $T = 120$ tape. Most machines these days have two or three recording and playback speeds. There is the SP or Standard Play mode, which will record and play two hours of programming on a T-120 tape. Then there is the LP or Long Play mode, which will record and play four hours of programming on a T-120 tape. More and more machines seem to be coming out with only the SP and the EP modes. These are acceptable, but you should definitely avoid buying a machine with *just* an SP mode. It will end up costing you more in additional tape than you might save on the purchase price. Furthermore, if it only records at one speed, it may only play back at one speed as well. So if you borrow or exchange tapes with friends and family that happen to be recorded on an LP or EP mode, the whole tape will look like on-screen search. Finally, it becomes more difficult to organize and store your tape library. For example, by using the EP mode I was able to get all eight hours of "Anne of Green Gables" on one of the newer T-160 tapes. On a one-speed machine I would have had to buy, use, label, and store *four* tapes.

Remote control. With a remote control your machine is easier to operate. Instead of hopping up and down to push the on-screen search, pause, and on/off buttons on the machine, you can control all those functions from your chair, the couch, or, in my older daughter's case, from the top of your blue and orange plastic slide. It is worth shopping around for a wireless remote. Doing away with one more tangled cord in the general area of the television and VCR is a real blessing, so unless the price difference is significant, I would go for the wireless version.

VHS or Beta. VHS machines are much more common, making tape renting, borrowing, and trading easier. Beta's picture quality may still be just a shade better, but not enough to make up for the inconvenience of having a machine that is incompatible with those of most of your neighbors.

Price. It is currently a buyer's world. VCRS are not terribly complex bits of technology by today's standards, so there are lots of decent machines available at very competitive prices. After you decide what features you need, shop for the machine that gives you those features for the best price, regardless of brand. Most of the machines are made by two Japanese companies which put different names on the cabinet, although the Korean companies are making a run at them.

A lot of retail outlets will push their service contracts at you. That is a hard call. My own experience persuades me not to buy them since we have never had anything go wrong with a VCR until we have had it for five or six years. However, we do not play many rental tapes and we keep the heads clean—something I advise you to do as well, using a wet, nonabrasive head-cleaning system. I have read reports, though, that a lot of VCRS do get sick, and that repair wards are full and slow. Most machines come with some type of warranty. I would use the machine heavily during that period to uncover and fix any major problems. Electronically the machines are pretty reliable; it is the mechanical elements that usually malfunction, so I would give the buttons etc. a thorough testing. I suppose it all comes down to a personal shopping decision based on, among other things, your personal appliance history. If things blow up on you, get the service contract. If your machines are nice to you, don't.

Cables and Satellites

The advent of cable television has had an amazing impact on the world of television. More than any other technological innovation, it has turned TV from a fair-sized stream into that mighty river of information that makes us a little uneasy, mesmerizes our children, and tantalizes our teenagers.

Cable is problematic because it offers us both Beauty and the Beast. My own bias is that I prefer not to live without Beauty, especially when the Beast is relatively easy to control. What's the Beauty of cable? Different things to different people, without a doubt. Our family finds Beauty in some of the children's offerings on Nickelodeon, a channel that is promoted as being "Just for Kids." We find Beauty on the Discovery Channel, which is full of travel shows, nature shows, and science shows; and "CNN Headline News," which enables us to catch a national news program whenever the children are down for naps or out in the yard. We have, on some cable systems, found Beauty in having two choices of PBS stations and a duplication of networks, which can insulate viewers from the rather bizarre whims of local station managers. It is also possible to stumble across Beauty on channels "up in the ether" whose names and numbers remain a mystery.

But the Beast trots along with Beauty on occasion. The Beast is most obvious in the structure of most cable systems. The various levels (called "tiers" in the industry) of service are seemingly randomly defined. The basic tier of service on our system gives me ESPN, the sports channel, and TBS (the Turner Broadcasting System) out of Atlanta, along with a Washington, D.C., station, the local network and PBS affiliates, a gaggle of UHF locals, and a couple of bulletin boards and C-Span. We find Beauty in none of these. So we are forced to go to the second tier of service, which costs more, in order to receive those things we wish to get from cable television.

This second tier of service does get us all those Beauties I mentioned earlier, but it drags MTV, VH-1, Shopping Channels, Midnight Mud-Wrestling, and a lot of other undesirables in along with it. But as I said earlier, we have decided that it is foolish to cut off your Beauty to spite the Beast—so we stay with cable. It allows us to exercise even greater control over what we watch because it greatly increases our options for both watching and taping.

Shopping for a Cable System

Shopping for a cable system is, in theory, a lot like shopping for a VCR. You decide what features you want and then shop for the best price. Unfortunately that theory runs up against a contrary reality. Cable companies, once they get the local franchise, tend to be the only game in town. So you look at what the company offers and decide if the price they want for their features is worth it to you.

Finding what the features are is sometimes more difficult than it sounds. The cable companies I have dealt with all seem to be under-staffed by underpaid college students working their way through school. If they know what the features of each tier of service are, they rarely seem to have time to tell you. This is a problem, especially for first-time cable customers who don't know an MTV from a CNN or an ESPN. A couple of suggestions:

Find a friend with cable. Find this friend and then go over to her house and camp out in front of the set for awhile. Ask her what the various stations show and take a look at it yourself. Talk to as many people as you can about the various cable options that they have. What they like, what they don't like. Do some personal market re-search.

Go to the cable company's office. Every cable company I have ever been to features a TV set in the lobby with its service being pumped into that set. Go up to the company representative, tell her you are interested in getting cable and that you would like written descrip-tions of the various tiers of service, and that you would like to sit there and watch examples of the programs. She will give you the written descriptions and will probably give you the remote control to change the channels on the lobby TV. Sit, browse, decide.

Fit your selections to your needs. As far as family programming is concerned, choices are still relatively limited. The Nickelodeon Chan-nel is a kid's channel of uneven quality that nevertheless is usually worth getting. It appears much of the time on second-tier services. The Disney Channel is just that. It is a premium channel for which you pay a specific fee per month. It provides some good programs, but we have never felt the monthly fee was worth the slight increase in quality children's fare—but then we have never gotten *any* premium channels for longer than the one-month free introductory offer that occasionally rolls around. I've already mentioned the advantages of "CNN Headline News" and the Discovery Channel, also usually sec-ond-tier services. Movie channels create more problems than they solve in the area of family viewing; if they are there, folks tend to watch them habitually, camping out in front of the tube in two-hour chunks.

In short, shopping for a cable service is often frustrating because it is so highly personalized, and the offerings keep shifting. But even given all that, it does increase viewing options and viewer control so significantly that I highly recommend you look into it.

I cannot say the same about satellite dishes, which enable you to receive direct microwave transmissions of TV signals. There are parts of the country where they can be valuable pieces of equipment, primarily in rural areas where neither cable nor broadcast signals are available. In those situations I can see considering the investment necessary to purchase a dish. However, in any other situation, the expense would seem to override the benefits, especially given the extent to which signals are now being "scrambled" to make them inaccessible to unlicensed satellite dish users. You can buy a TV, a VCR, and a couple of hundred prerecorded videotapes for the cost of a dish.

It is a brave new world that has such gizmos in it. But the new technology of television—VCRs and cable systems—has in many ways given us, as consumers, more control over the impact television has on our lives and our families than we have ever had before.

Video Co-ops

Controlling the technology for our benefit is a goal we can all agree on, but the best way to go about it is not always clear. There is a wide range of viewer organizations that ebb and flow out there along the electronic river; organizations that seek to get rid of this kind of program, or ban that kind of channel, or label this particular video. I must admit that I find those kinds of attempts to control the media misdirected, and perhaps more harmful than the messages they seek to curtail.

The health of our society is reflected in the quality of the decisions we freely make, not in the quality of the decisions that we force upon others. As concerned consumers of television we need to concentrate on making good choices, and on maximizing the amount of quality programming available for our choosing. We also need to concentrate on maximizing our own resources; video hardware and video cassettes are less expensive than they used to be, but they are still not cheap. The most effective way to accomplish these ends is to form a video co-op.

A video co-op is an organization of parents, friends, neighbors, coworkers, or whoever else is interested in seeking video needs and concerns by sharing resources, information, and experiences. Let's talk about some of the possibilities in each of those areas.

Sharing Resources

The single piece of equipment that gives you the most control over your television is a VCR. There is a paradoxical relationship between who can benefit most from VCRs and who can best afford them. Television has long been the major diversion of the American blue-collar worker. *The International Television and Video Almanac* reports that as education and income decrease, television viewing goes up. In short, economically disadvantaged folks in America watch a lot of TV. And the same is true of their children. But, and here is the paradox, it is those children who are most poorly served by network TV. I mean, while their folks are out desperately searching for ways to make ends meet, the kids are home watching the tube, learning that the rest of the kids won't like them unless they wear $60.00 jeans, $50.00 sunglasses, and $40.00 sneakers. Thanks a lot Madison Avenue.

This group of kids and their families can certainly benefit from restricting the amount of network fare that they watch and bringing some more beneficial video into their home via a VCR. This group of families also tends to be the group least able to afford a VCR. Video co-ops can help you meet the expense of a VCR in a couple of ways.

First, I am aware of co-ops that have actually pooled their resources and bought one VCR at at time until each family had one; however, unless you happen to have the wisdom of Solomon running your group I would not really advise that strategy. You might want to consider this option instead. Go to each major dealer in your area, tell them you are a video co-op and are interested in buying three or six or eight machines from them. What is the best price they can offer you? How long will that price be good?

Once you have cut your best deal, everyone in the co-op goes into high-gear fund-raising. You have bake sales, the children have car washes, you collect newspapers and returnable bottles, you give up smoking or beer or pizza for a week and put the money in the pot. You go to your place of worship, or your school, or the Y to get other suggestions for fund-raising. You will be amazed what several motivated families can accomplish.

If even the best deal you can find is out of your price range, go ahead and do your fund-raising without a deal. Then begin to shop the want ads, the repair shops, and the large outlet service departments for used machines. As high-tech fans trade up for the latest set of bells and whistles and computer-controlled digital sound, you can pick up their perfectly good old machines for prices far below retail.

The second major resource we need to have in order to control television in our lives is videotapes. The dominant function of most video co-ops is to borrow, trade, and exchange tapes. The logistics get a little complicated, but a couple of systems work fairly well.

The central library system works best if everyone lives fairly close to each other. A spare closet, a cabinet in a garage, or a bookcase in the playroom becomes the library. Here the co-op stores its circulating tapes, and members come over to check the tapes out and return them. With this system you need to pay particular attention to the care and feeding of the librarian. Some folks like the job. It gives them a chance to see co-op members quite often, and there is the advantage of having the library right there when you want to use it. On the other hand, it can be inconvenient with people coming in and out and kids always getting into the tapes. A specific term of office or a rotation system helps minimize the disadvantages of the librarian's life.

A second system is to keep a list of all the tapes that the co-op has and where they "live." Members then arrange to check tapes out from one another. The list gets updated at periodic meetings of the cooperative. It is a less personal system, but it gets the job done.

Library acquisitions is another area in which a co-op can make our video life easier. Some co-ops set up a dues structure that allows for the purchase of prerecorded tapes. Others just assume that people will contribute resources according to their abilities. A co-op makes off-the-air taping much easier. A major problem in off-the-air taping is that machines (and, of course, the people who program them) do not do what they are supposed to. Hence, you walk out of your house not really 100 percent sure that you will return to find that the program you are dying to see has been taped. With a co-op there is almost always someone planning to be home the night that program A, or B, or C is going to air. That person then becomes the co-op's official VCR babysitter for the night, making sure the program gets taped, editing out commercials, etc. A co-op also lets you tape more than one program at the same time, since it has multiple machines at its disposal. So when the networks decide to run two or three good shows opposite each other, the co-op can get them all.

Video co-ops can aid us in our efforts to control the quality of television in our lives by allowing us to share or coordinate the use of resources like VCRs and videotapes. But co-ops can be equally valuable in the simple sharing of information.

Sharing Information

As I have mentioned earlier, writing this book has made me very aware of the bewildering variety of programming out there—on the air and on tape—that is labeled "children's programming," or "family programming," or "young adult programming." Some of it is excellent and some of it is garbage. A video co-op helps the group become aware of good new programs without everyone's having to wade through all the garbage to find it.

In addition to information about specific new programs, a video co-op allows members to share information about sources of new programming. Maybe one member stumbles across a new bookstore with good children's video offerings; someone else gets on a mailing list from a company specializing in quality videos for young adolescents;

a third discovers a pawn shop with good used VCRs. All this information can enhance your ability to control television in your home, and
the co-op increases your access to the information.

Some co-ops use newsletters to share information, others share the
information at formal co-op meetings, and still others use the coffee
klatch as an information-sharing session. The way you organize your
group will determine the format you use to share information.

Sharing Experiences

As in all aspects of parenting, or otherwise coordinating the work-
ings of a family, when you try to control the impact of television on
your family, some things work and some things don't. The secret to
success is often not finding that one magical answer to your problems;
but rather getting exposed to enough possible answers that one—or a
combination of several—works for you.

The video co-op can enable you to share ideas about curtailing
viewing, blunting the impact of advertising, setting up media probe
sessions as part of a sleep-over, etc. But try not to let the co-op become
an organization where you sit around and talk exclusively about "kids
and television." Instead of regarding family members as passive re-
cipients of information gained from the co-op, involve the whole
family in co-op activities and give as much responsibility as you can to
the kids. In that way the co-op can help teach our kids to control
television in their lives.

Influencing the Industry

I like comic strips—that should be fairly obvious. I think they often
provide delightfully succinct bits of insight into the world around us. I
recall, but sadly cannot find, an old Pogo strip that ends with Pogo's
looking out of the final panel saying, "We have met the enemy, and
they is us!" That is the way it is with television programming.

As we mentioned before, the networks, having for the most part
been bought up by some mega-conglomerate or another, don't really
try to produce bad programs. They simply want to make a profit by
either producing or purchasing and airing the programs that will
result in the largest audiences—or greatest revenues—for the company. It is our viewing patterns that have told them to produce and air
the kinds of programs we now see on television. Video co-ops can
have an impact upon that process.

Let us return to the basic premise underlying programming decisions. The larger the audience for a program, and hence the higher the
ratings, the greater the advertising rate that can be charged for advertising slots within that program. We need to keep several things in

mind as we consider how to use this formula to the advantage of the video co-op and the individual family.

First, the network really does not care who *isn't* watching any particular program, but they care very much about who and how many people *are* watching their programs. Secondly, the advent of the people-meter (see Chapter 1) has made the networks a little uncertain about the accuracy of their audience-measuring methods.

These two items strongly suggest the following strategy for getting the kind of programming you want. Don't waste your energy trying to get rid of programs you do not like. If lots of other people want to watch them, your protests and boycotts will not affect the networks—and probably should not. Instead, pour all your energy into supporting those programs you wish to see continued. Supportive letters from significant numbers of viewers may well save programs with marginal ratings—depending on whom you believe, letter-writing campaigns have helped save the likes of "Cagney and Lacy," "FAME," "St. Elsewhere," and "Little House on the Prairie."

To whom do you write? Well, I am a great believer in writing to the very top of the organization. If that is not where programming decisions get made, it is at least where the final responsibility for them lies, and it is where praise may do the most good. So, I suggest that you write to the following people to drum up support for your favorite programs:

For ABC:
Mr. Daniel Burke
President and C.E.O.
Capital Cities/ABC Inc.
1330 Avenue of the Americas
New York, New York 10019

For CBS:
Mr. Laurence Tisch
President and C.E.O.
CBS Inc.
51 W. 52 Street
New York, New York 10019

For Fox:
Mr. Barry Diller
Chairman and C.E.O.
Fox Broadcasting Company
10201 W. Pico Blvd.
Los Angeles, California 90035

For NBC:
Mr. Robert Wright
President and C.E.O.
National Broadcasting Co., Inc.
30 Rockefeller Plaza
New York, New York 10112

For PBS:
Mr. Bruce L. Christensen
President and C.E.O.
Public Broadcasting Service
1320 Braddock Place
Alexandria, Virginia 22314

Write what you feel, clearly and concisely. There are two standard forms which allow you to express what you feel about a program without that sterile, formula, letter-writing-campaign feel to them. They go sort of like this.

In Praise of a Good Show

Dear ———:

I just wanted to drop you a quick note to let you know how much our family enjoys your program ———. It has become a regular part of our [whatever day] and when we can't be home we always try to tape it.

We particularly enjoy—[you fill in what it is that you particularly enjoy in this paragraph.]

We don't usually watch much TV, but might be tempted to if more programs of this quality were available. I know you don't get a lot of praise when you do something right, so thanks again—this time you definitely did something right!!

Sincerely,

The Soft Complaint

Dear ———:

I try to drop you a note when I see something I like on your network, and I wish this could be one of those notes—but it isn't. I felt I had to write to tell you how disappointed our family was in your program ———.

We were particularly bothered by ———.

This program doesn't measure up to the standards you set for yourself with [fill in the name of a laudable program from the network—there's probably one in there somewhere. This paragraph is the place where you want to make yet another plug for the programs that you do enjoy. If you can't find a really good program to praise on this network, praise one from another network. Networks don't care whom they copy.] We'll try to check in on your other offerings from time to time. Hope they are better than this one.

Sincerely,

I would encourage you to write often, and as an individual. You might want to send a letter signed by the co-op, but don't let the co-op letter stand alone. With networks it is always a numbers game, whether it be the number of viewers or the number of letters. But I sincerely believe we are coming into an age in the television industry when significant numbers of personal letters from thoughtful viewers may come to play an increasingly larger role in the programming decision-making process—especially if those letters support trends obvious in more traditional audience data.

Finally, although the local network affiliate is often merely a conduit for network programs, you should not overlook local station managers in your letter-writing efforts. Local input is important for two reasons. First, some local stations do still produce some children's programs, and they should be encouraged and guided in those efforts. Second, local affiliates do talk to their networks, and you want them to know how you feel about their programs so that they can report those perceptions to the folks at the network—the people who decide what programs live and what programs die.

Viewer Organizations

There is a significant difference between video co-ops and most professional, national viewer organizations. Video co-ops are small neighborhood organizations whose members seek to make the wisest decisions possible about the video that they allow into their homes. Most viewer organizations—at least the ones that I get mailings from—are lobbying organizations that are attempting to suppress some kind of message or another.

While these groups strike out at this message or that message as being antifamily, or antichurch, or sexist, or racist, they somehow fail to see that the presence of bad messages is one of the inevitabilities of living in a free society. These "anti-something" viewer organizations attempt to use their freedom of expression to deny someone else the right to express themselves. I am too much of a constitutional conservative to get into that kind of activity. Furthermore, from the perspective of a pragmatic parent, it doesn't do much good. Bad messages stay in the marketplace until the *public or consumer demand* for those messages decreases to the point where it is no longer profitable to produce them. In short, bad programs will go away when audiences no longer ask for them. That challenges us to teach our children good media consumption skills. When we do that we will shrink the profit potential for bad programs to the point where the garbage on TV will become as rare as a good cartoon on Saturday morning is today.

There is, however, one viewer organization that I can support wholeheartedly—Action for Children's Television. This organization is not anti-anything. It is pro-quality children's programming. The difference is not merely a question of language. Action for Children's Television (ACT) is a national advocate for the child audience. It seeks to make sure that advertisers follow the existing laws in regard to children's television, and it serves as a watchdog on the FCC when it attempts to change those laws. It attempts to maximize the amount of quality programming available to kids. For more information about ACT write to:

Ms. Peggy Charren, President
Action for Children's Television
20 University Road
Cambridge, Massachusetts 02138

We need to keep in mind that the television industry is a business that provides goods and services in order to generate profits. Our responsibility as consumers is to utilize those goods and services in ways that meet the needs and wishes of our family. Sometimes we do that alone, sometimes through a neighborhood video co-op, and sometimes with a little help from our friends—like the good folks at ACT. But however you choose to assert yourself as an intelligent consumer of television, remember to let the industry know what you think. Be lavish in your praise and loud in your objections. You see, the television industry is a lot like the mule in the old story—"It'll do what you tell it to do; but sometimes you have to hit it with a two-by-four to get its attention."

6

You Make the Difference

We have spent five chapters now describing how best to utilize the messages and machinery of contemporary television. We have talked about the pitfalls and the benefits of today's video technology. We have discussed the possible impact of television on our family's values, and we have examined parasocial relationships—those strange relationships that grow up between "characters" and "real people."

We have talked about a lot of things that pertain to us, our children, our families, and the high-tech house guest that moved in somehow when we were not really paying that much attention. All of those chapters and discussions contain—I sincerely believe—important and helpful bits of information. Still, the issues we need to discuss in this chapter may well be more important than any that have preceded them, because they involve teaching our children how *not* to watch television, how *not* to learn from the media.

Television is a lot like dessert. It is basically a sugar-based product. Some desserts contain fruit or milk products and can—in moderation—actually be beneficial to our development, for both nutritional and psychological reasons. But, more usually, desserts are high in sugar, fat, calories, and cholesterol. In short, dessert tastes good but isn't very good for us.

The odds are that we are not going to give up dessert, either for ourselves or for our children. Therefore we attempt to make sure that our other nutritional habits make up for the excesses of our desserts.

The analogy holds for television. We probably will not give it up either—like dessert, it likely meets some important needs. But our major focus should be making sure that other experiences in our lives overwhelm the potential negative excesses of television. As I mentioned in Chapter 4, children often see television as presenting options for their futures. The fictions of television do not actually become reality, but they do become models for how reality might be. As parents we need to attempt to provide alternatives to this TV-screen view of the world. We do that by providing experiences in fiction and reality that are richer and more rewarding than those offered by television.

Experiences in Fiction

Television is merely the latest in a long line of purveyors of mass entertainment. But the entertainment media have moved, step by step, away from the reality they originally depicted and away from the active, dynamic relationship that once existed between the storyteller and the audience.

The first "plays" were probably "news stories," vivid presentations at a fireside that depicted how the evening's meal made the dramatic transition from large beast to hunk of meat. Audience members and storytellers were probably one and the same, with all members of the group chiming in with their own versions of the event. As time moved on the plays became more formalized, with clearer distinctions made between who spoke and who listened. The audience became the chorus, who responded en masse, but still within the context of the play. Then the chorus was shoved off the stage into seats, and the passive audience was born.

Film took the next step, temporally separating the actors and the audience and making it possible for many different groups of people to watch the same presentation at different times. But the "activity" of a large audience remained. People still laughed together as a group, fell silent as a group, and—at least when I was a kid—applauded as a group at the end of the performance.

Television provides the ultimate opportunity for passivity. Like film, it separates the audience and the performer; but unlike film, it isolates the individual audience member. The solitary viewer alone in a room, an expressionless face illuminated by the flickering images of the TV screen—this has become the icon of alienation for our age.

We have already seen that it does not have to be that way. In Chapter 3 we discussed how kids, even while watching TV, show an inclination for action. We still possess that ancient desire to be part of the process, not merely observers. As parents we need to walk our kids back down the road a bit, share with them the days when audience and actor were one—and show them that the experiences of those days can be continued today.

The first medium we need to explore with them is the one from which all but the very earliest of performances have sprung—the written word.

Reprinted by permission of Tribune Media Services.

Experiences in Reading

At first blush, reading may seem to be just as passive an activity as television. What is the difference between a child glued to the tube and a child immersed in a book? There is literally a world of difference. When children watch television they are observing a world that someone else has created from a written script—they are observing the end product of someone else's creative interpretation of literature. When children read books, or have books read to them, *they create*. They paint the sets, design the costumes, cast the characters—all in that wonderful theater inside their heads.

As a parent you can give your child no greater gift than the love of reading. I grade lots of papers from college students, and I can easily tell you what papers come from students who have grown up reading for enjoyment, and what papers do not. Children who read well, who read for enjoyment, write well. Well-read students have an intuitive feel for sentence structure, for grammar, for language. They are more successful, in my classes, and most others I'll warrant, than students who have not been taught to love reading.

When do you start reading to your kids? Well, I remember a fascinating conversation I had with a woman who swore that her parents had read *War and Peace* to her while she was still in utero, which she claimed had had an amazing impact upon her life. Her experience notwithstanding, I think that waiting until the child is born is quite acceptable. But I wouldn't wait much longer.

We started reading to both our children in the first few days of their lives. No, we don't think they understood the stories or were able to identify the pictures. But they did come to associate the whole ritual of reading—the sound of a voice, the turning of a book's pages—with being cuddled and full and happy. Some babies take to being read to more readily than others. Our older girl, Andrea, would listen to stories from the very beginning. As a matter of fact, she was a very active child, and reading was the one thing that would slow her down. She will still listen to stories for as long as you will read to her. My mother has read to her for literally hours at a stretch.

The baby, who is now about two years old, was different. She would push the books away and go look for a toy, or just fuss. But my wife continued to make reading part of the nap and bedtime rituals, and at about nine months Emily began to pay attention. Now she, like her sister before her, hauls her books around the house with her other favorite toys.

Reading is not my area of expertise, other than as a consumer, but let me offer these two specific bits of advice: (1) read to your children every day, even after they can read; (2) go out today and buy, or check out of the library, a book called *The Read-Aloud Handbook* by Jim Trelease, a Penguin Handbook costing about $7.00. It will be one of the best $7.00 you ever spend. Trelease is without doubt the Drs. Spock and Brazelton of reading to and with children. He addresses in great detail the issues of what, when, and how.

Experiences in Theater

As I have mentioned several times in this book, Andrea does not sit still. Whether I am reading to her, or she is watching TV, she is in motion—unless she is sick. There is one other exception to that Andrea axiom. I first noticed it when she was four years old. Some friends of ours invited Andrea to the dress rehearsal of a musical version of *Cinderella* that they were doing for the local community theater. Andrea and I went together. We sat down, and she began to wiggle and bounce, greeting her friends and commenting on everyone else in the theater. But finally the curtain went up and the music began—and Andrea sat transfixed for ninety minutes. I would occasionally put my arm around her to make sure she was breathing. It was truly amazing. And the experience has been repeated several times since; *Peter Pan* and a local rehearsal for a musical review both had the same effect. There is something magical about the theater—that transcends the most elaborate electronic special effects of television. The idea that there are live human beings up there acting out a story is entrancing.

As a result of these experiences we enrolled Andrea in a class at the local art center called "Fairy Tale Theater." There she and fifteen or twenty other stage-struck kindergartners and first-graders acted out fairy tales under the guidance of a very gentle director/teacher. The benefits have been varied. Andrea has learned some new ways to express herself. And we have gained a new tool in helping her correct her behavior. When Andrea is having trouble behaving as we would like her to, we say: "Let's play that scene again." She then leaves the area of the confrontation for as long as she needs to "get into character." Then when she enters the scene, we play it again, leaving the anger and frustration back in the first scene. It works quite often and quite well.

Theater, live theater, is wonderful for children, and many communities have active children's theater programs. Some provide plays for children to watch and some provide workshops that help kids put on plays of their own. I strongly urge you to check out those opportunities.

Experiences in Storytelling

The old craft of storytelling is enjoying a rejuvenation in America. In libraries, at art shows, at fairs and picnics, at children's festivals—in hundreds of places all around the country a new breed of storyteller is reviving one of the most ancient forms of literature. We have been to several storytelling events and they are wonderful. Folktales from every region of the country and the world come alive in the voices of these talented performers. Many of them blend songs and dance into the telling of the tale, while some draw the audience into an active role. Workshops are often part of the event, giving the storytellers an opportunity to share the details of their craft and point interested people to new resources, new stories. Storytelling is a delightful, experiential trip into literature.

It is easy to see that the more passive modes of experiencing fiction—film and television—are far from the only ways to involve our family in the world of literature. Reading, theater, and storytelling are three of many other ways of getting more actively involved in literature, fiction, and entertainment. The important thing is to get into the pipeline of information that tells you about these kinds of activities.

I would suggest that you start with your public library. They often sponsor events of this type, and surely have information about events going on in the community. The children's librarian in particular is often an excellent source of information on children's theater and storytelling events. I would also find out whether or not your community has an Arts Council or a Cultural Activities Board. If so, get on the mailing list. If your community does not have an Arts Council, you might want to consider becoming that council or board yourself! Radio and television stations that are affiliated with PBS also tend to be good sources of information about these kinds of cultural events. It may take some effort to get involved with these more active literary experiences, but you and your children will be glad you made the effort.

Experiences in Reality

Adventures into literature and the arts are valuable, but they are still secondary in importance to our family's experiences in reality. Literature, after all, is not the world—it is someone's interpretation and depiction of the world. The reality of our world is how we interact with each other. It is an old adage but true—we teach our children primarily by our own behavior. Our example of how to live life is more important to our children than anything the media can present to them, and we need to try to match what we believe with what we model. We may tell our children, "Do what I say, not what I do." But chances are they will do as we do.

Experiences in the Family

Our values—our attitudes toward love and trust, sex and violence, and consumerism—are primarily defined by behaviors in the home. If we wish our children to be trusting and loving, then we need to trust them and love them, even when they do not do very lovable things. We correct, we show disappointment, but we continue to trust and we continue to love. We give them a hug before we send them to time-out or to their rooms. We tell them, sincerely, that we wish we did not have to keep them home from this friend's house or that friend's party—but that we have to, or they will never remember how to behave, and soon they will not have any friends. We love and we trust even as we discipline and correct.

If we wish to blunt the media's message of easy sex and casual, callous relationships, then we need to treat our partners with tenderness and compassion. It is in the home that children learn most about human relationships. Children learn how to treat people by the way they are treated, and by the way they see others treated in their home—that is reality, that is how the world works.

The same is true with violence. The central issue that lies behind violence is the premise that if you are bigger and stronger, if you control more power, you can force people to do what you want. We cannot try to teach children, on the one hand, that might *does not* make right, if the other hand smacks their bottoms for every minor infringement of the household code. We cannot teach them to reason out their differences if Mom and Dad resolve theirs by flinging the dishes at one another—or worse.

Children also learn their parents' patterns of consumption. We cannot teach our children to ignore the appeals of Madison Avenue if they see patterns of conspicuous consumption around them every day. We cannot teach them that people are unique and precious in their own right if our discussions of our friends and peers center on how they look, what they have bought, how big their houses are, or how much money they make.

Children learn about how families work, about how people behave toward one another, by watching how their families work and how their parents treat them and each other.

Experiences in Work and Society

Similarly, children learn about their roles in and attitudes about work and society from watching their parents. If we wish to teach children that the value of work is the service or product produced, and the feeling of accomplishment that lies behind that process, then we need to demonstrate that by our own behavior and attitudes. It is not the message I am getting in my classroom. A few weeks ago I gave an address at a dinner for the members of an academic honorary society. I spoke to the graduates about their obligation to make the world a better place, about the notion that success is not measured by a pay-check. I was warmly applauded, and many of the students expressed their appreciation of my message. But not more than twenty minutes later I overheard the following conversation.

> He: So what are you doing after graduation?
> She: I'm going down to Atlanta, I've got a job with "mumble,
> mumble" [I'd tell you, but I couldn't hear].
> He: What are you going to do for them?
> She: If they'll pay me enough I'll do anything they want.
> Both: Ha, ha.

I didn't join in their laughter. Now, I'm not saying that a parent or family can be held completely responsible for the goals and ideals of their college graduate children, but I am saying that the home has more potential to shape the child's values than any other socializing agent, and that we need to maximize the impact of our example.

If we wish to teach our children that they have an obligation to their society, then we need to demonstrate our own feelings of social obliga-tion. We need to adopt a charity or a service organization or a social action project as our cause. We need to demonstrate the kinds of behaviors that we feel are appropriate for a concerned, active citizen.

Experiences in Recreation

Finally, we need to demonstrate specific alternatives to passive use of leisure time. We cannot berate our kids for not playing outside if we are sprawled on the couch with a beer watching the thirty-fourth NBA play-off game. *I* realize that you have worked hard all week, and *I* realize that these actually are the finals. The problem is that odds are *your kid* doesn't realize that—and no amount of explaining is going to make that point clear. What they see is someone saying, "Do what I say, not what I do."

If we want our kids to pursue active, healthy recreation, then we need to model that kind of behavior ourselves, no matter how much it hurts. So check with the video co-op and see if someone can tape the game (I never said that co-ops had to operate exclusively for the kids!) and begin to explore some options in recreation.

For those of you who haven't seen organized recreation since Y camp in junior high school, watch out—there has been somewhat of a revolution out there. I am certainly not the person to apprise you of the specifics of that revolution—up until last year I was still under the impression that a "T-ball" was something that went into a "Jotter" to make the ink flow. Besides, Andrea is an active member of the swim team (I do, at least, swim laps during practice) and the baby just started to walk!

But there are lots of people out there who can give you the scoop on everything from family hiking groups, through mini-triathlons, to Frisbee tournaments. Again, I would start with your local city, town, or county government and see about the local recreation department. From there I would check out bulletins posted at sporting goods stores, parks, local swim clubs, city pools, your church or synagogue, or the Y for announcements about local recreation group meetings and activities. If that fails, go to the trusty library for books on family recreation, new games, and leisure activities and start your own recreation group—maybe with your video co-op!

In the final analysis, you are the most dominant role model for your family. If you want the world that your child lives in to reflect the values of your family, then make very, very sure that the world you construct with your family reflects those values. Children behave, for the most part, as they are taught to behave. Make sure that you as a family are modeling the behaviors you want to teach.

Children did not invent racism, or sexism, or religious intolerance. Children did not invent abusive spouses or substance abuse. Children were not even the first to watch television. Couch potatoes aren't born; they grow only in an environment conducive to the species.

Children mimic what they see around them. Children can probably be taught not to watch television, but only if you decide not to watch TV too. If you make that decision, please pass this book on to someone who is going to keep his or her set. If, on the other hand, you decide to view wisely rather than not at all, remember that one of the most important things you can teach your children about television is that *there are lots of things in the world that are more fun than watching it!*

7

Tomorrow's Memories: Some of the Best in Children's Television

I think we all have memories of meaningful or idyllic experiences that we would like to recreate for our children. For me, several of those memories involve reading. The Public Library in Stockton, California, is a place I remember well. My father had a summer teaching position at the University of the Pacific and the library took the place of the friends we had left behind in Ohio. It was there that I was introduced to Thornton Burgess's *Mother West Wind Books. Little Joe the Otter* was my favorite, and I can still see the simple, engaging illustrations in my mind's eye. A few years later it was a camp on the shores of Lake Michigan where my parents would rent a cabin for a week or two during the summer. We kids would rush from the breakers across the hot sand and throw ourselves into the shade of Dad's lean-to. Mom would unpack her picnic lunch and we would all dig the books out of the beach bag. It was in this setting that I first read the Rover Boys series, a seemingly endless adolescent adventure series my mother had saved from her own childhood.

I also remember my first personally planned literary extravaganza. We lived in Europe during my fifth- and sixth-grade years, and I fell in love with *The Adventures of Sherlock Holmes*. When it came time to return to the States I soon discovered that we would sail across the English Channel, take the train to Southampton, and from there sail home to America. It was an ideal opportunity for the perfect reading of Sherlock Holmes.

The day of the channel crossing dawned gray and rainy—I was thrilled. Immediately upon boarding the ferry I hauled a deck chair off to the most deserted portion of the ship. There I spent a glorious day bundled against the mist, listening to fog horns, occasionally leaning out across the rail and staring, piercingly I hoped, into the gloom toward England. The rest of the time I was immersed in the exploits of the greatest consulting detective the world has ever known.

The fact that none of these memories is a television memory does not mean that the medium is incapable of similar impact. It is, rather, an indication of the almost total absence of good children's programming during my childhood. The same is not true for children growing up today. There are many excellent television experiences available for our children, and I know that my daughters will combine video *and* literary experiences when they recall favorite stories from their childhood.

The problem is one of discrimination and profit. When I was growing up there was little profit in bad books for children. If the story was not at least mildly engaging, if the illustrations did not hold the attention, the book never made it to a second printing and you did not have to worry about it. Today, as we discussed in Chapter 3, there can be a lot of profit in bad television shows for children. The program-length commercial has flooded television with bad but profitable programs that are undeserving of any place in a child's memory. So one is faced with the task of discriminating between the good, the bad, and the merely mediocre.

I have said before that I do not like telling people what is good TV and what is bad TV for their families. That's not really true—if it were I wouldn't have written this book. But what is true is that my opinion is only my opinion—or rather our opinion, since television analysis is a family process in our household. But our favorites are a reflection of our family's values, as yours should be. We may love programs your family might wish to throw things at—and vice versa. But nonetheless a list of "good" programs is something all parents seem to want. This last chapter is my attempt to address that desire.

The exploding market in children's television made covering all the available material virtually impossible, so I will explain the process of selection and organization for each division of material as we go along. First of all, when confronted with the world of children's video, I decided it was logical to divide the offerings according to whether they were video cassette programs—those programs available for purchase or rental on video cassette; broadcast programs—those programs than any receiver can pick up; and cable programs—those programs available on most cable systems. I need to point out that these categories are not mutually exclusive. Some programs that started out on cable have been picked up by PBS, and some old programs are carried by both cable stations and broadcast independents (often UHF stations), and so on. However, I have tried to cover the noteworthy programs to the best of my ability.

Video Cassette Programs

The process I followed in reviewing video cassette offerings was slightly different from the process I employed in the broadcast and cable sections. In this area I realized that I could not hope just to stumble across even a reasonable cross section of the wide variety of tapes currently available for the children's market. So I wrote to as many companies as I could asking them to send me what they considered their best children's tapes for review and inclusion in this portion of the book. The following companies responded.

Participating Companies

Buena Vista Home Video
cbs/Fox Children's Videos
Children's Circle Video
Children's Video Library
Children's Play Video (cpv, Inc.)
Embassy Home Entertainment
Family Home Entertainment
rca/Columbia Pictures Home Video
Hi-Tops Video
Little People Video
Lorimar Home Video
Magic Windows
Media Home Entertainment
Nelson Entertainment
New World Video
Pacific Arts Video
Paramount Home Video
Playhouse Video
Rabbit Ears Productions
Random House Home Video
Scholastic-Lorimar
Snoopy's Home Video Library
Sony Video Software
Vestron Video
Walt Disney Home Video
Warner Home Video

I would like to express my sincere thanks to these companies. They knew, I am sure, that the author of a book on television viewing and the family might not feel that the programming they were offering was "good" programming for children. As the following reviews indicate, sometimes they were right. However, they still had the courage to submit their work for review, and I thank them for that.

A small number of companies I contacted were unable to participate, for one reason or another. I hope in future editions of this work to be able to include reviews of their tapes as well.

The listing will follow the traditional "Four Star" method of evaluation, except, of course, I will use a "Four TVs" system. Also, I have rated each tape for four different age ranges, since the appropriateness and appeal of the tapes vary according to the age of the viewer. The age ranges are:

TV Babies	birth to 2 years
TV Toddlers	2 to 5 years
TV Kids	5 to 11 years
River Riders	11 and older

The ratings are:

☐ ☐ ☐ ☐ = wonderful
☐ ☐ ☐ = really good
☐ ☐ = above average
☐ = mediocre
☒ = pass on this one

I included prices when they were sent to me. However, you need to realize that those were 1988 prices and *not* sale prices—so shop, shop, shop. You will see some strange combinations listed as company names. Things like Sony/Rabbit Ears Productions. That means that Sony distributes the tape, but it was produced by Rabbit Ears Productions. I am giving you both names because, should you choose to order the tape from your local bookstore or video outlet, it is helpful to have as much information as possible.

Children's Video Reviews

Across the Great Divide 102 min.

Media Home Entertainment

birth to 2 years	☒	5 to 11 years	☐ ☐ ☐
2 to 5 years	☒	11 and older	☐ ☐ ☐

This story is set in the American West of 1876. Two orphans, living in the East, have inherited four hundred acres in Salem, Oregon, but they need to get there by a certain date or they will forfeit their inheritance. This requirement forces them into an uneasy alliance with a con-artist on the lam.

An endearing cast of characters features the spunky older sister, her slightly blood-thirsty little brother, the flim-flam man, a well-depicted branch of the Blackfoot Nation, and some delightful villains. The script makes a number of concessions to the period, resulting in some nice linguistic nuances that will broaden your children's vocabulary. The photography is well done and the music—while sometimes longer than the children would like—adds a nice touch. For my money this is the best of the "wilderness adventure" tapes I looked at.

The Adventures of the Wilderness Family 100 min.
Wilderness Family: Part 2 104 min.
Mountain Family Robinson 102 min.

Media Home Entertainment

birth to 2 years ⊠		5 to 11 years 🖵 🖵
2 to 5 years ⊠		11 and older 🖵 🖵

These three tapes really fooled me. The various scenes with wolves, mountain lions, and renegade grizzly bears immediately took them off the list for my kids because of their potential for causing nightmares. So I shipped them out to my more aggressive eight- to twelve-year-old reviewers, and they loved them!

The tapes tell the story—called true on the first two tapes and a "moving drama" on the third—of a family who gets totally fed up with life in Los Angeles and moves lock, stock, barrel, and dog to Alaskan mountains so wild they are accessible only to bush pilots.

The acting is uneven, the photography is quite nice, the stories are a tad disjointed and stretch credibility many times—but as I said for a certain audience these tapes apparently are just the ticket.

Animal Alphabet 30 min.

Scholastic-Lorimar

birth to 2 years 🖵 🖵		5 to 11 years 🖵
2 to 5 years 🖵 🖵		11 and older ⊠

This tape assigns an animal to every letter of the alphabet—no, "X" is for ox, but I can't think of an X animal either. Then the tape devotes an original song and a short film clip to each animal. The tape will probably not teach a child either about the alphabet or the animals, but the photography and the music are well done enough to make the tape a nice review for both. It is also a good quiet-time tape as the music and film clips are both pleasantly mellow.

In defense of the "X is for ox" sequence, the tape goes to great length to point out that "X" *ends* ox. Also "U" is for unicorn, "an imaginary animal."

Arte Johnson's Kids Stuff 19 min.

Embassy Home Entertainment

birth to 2 years	&#9746;	5 to 11 years	☐ ☐
2 to 5 years	&#9744;	11 and older,	☐ ☐

My last exposure to Arte Johnson was listening to him say "Verrry interesting—but stoopid!" on "Rowan and Martin's Laugh-In." However, this tape is very interesting and not at all stupid. The nineteen-minute length should not put you off—it is not a story tape, but rather an instructional tape in which Mr. Johnson explores the building of toys at home using things that can be found around the house—milk cartons, shoe boxes, paper bags, tape, straws, cardboard tubes, crayons, scissors—you know, basic "cut, fold, and paste" stuff. Many of the toys he creates make you say, "I could have thought of that!" And we probably could have—given five minutes of peace and another cup of coffee. But if those niceties are as rare around your house as they are around ours, this tape can really come in handy.

Baby Animals Just Want to Have Fun 30 min.

Scholastic-Lorimar

birth to 2 years	☐ ☐ ☐	5 to 11 years	☐ ☐
2 to 5 years	☐ ☐ ☐	11 and older	&#9746;

This is one of those perfect tapes for young children—as young as you wish. What Scholastic Lorimar has done is blend some cute footage of baby animals—and an occasional human—with music and some stories. Hortense, the baby rabbit, explores the world around her hole and meets cows, turtles, turkeys, puppies. We hear a song about kittens and see the story of Raindance, the shy little pony. Next Peter Puppy shows his perfect present. My Little Chickadee is a cute music video about baby chicks. After that the skunk children come over to find a home. The title tune is next and accompanies shots of baby animals "just having fun." The conclusion features more of the same.

This tape seems to enthrall the little ones, and it is excellent for teaching them animal names. It is a good buy.

Baby Animals in the Wild 30 min.

Lorimar Home Video

birth to 2 years	☐	☐	☐	5 to 11 years	☐	☐
2 to 5 years	☐	☐	☐	11 and older	☒	

An equally endearing companion piece to *Baby Animals Just Want to Have Fun*, this tape shows us baby wild animals instead of domestic animals. The appeal of these two tapes is reflected in the fact that for a couple of months around her second birthday my youngest daughter would watch little else on tape—some "Sesame Street," and a little "Mr. Rogers," but for the most part it was "Animals, Daddy, Animals, Mommy." An invaluable set of tapes for ear infection days!

Banjo: The Woodpile Cat 30 min.

Children's Video Library

birth to 2 years	☒	5 to 11 years	☐
2 to 5 years	☐	11 and older	☒

You do not often find animation of this quality in a thirty-minute tape. The box touts it as being animated in the classic Disney tradition, and it is. It is an engaging story of Banjo, a little cat who just cannot behave. He eventually runs away from home to the city. There he meets new friends and encounters a series of adventures and misadventures that convince him that home is where he really wants to be.

I have a little trouble with the fact that Banjo appears to remain a fairly unrepentant little juvenile delinquent, even after returning home. But some "directed interpretation" on the part of the astute parent can blunt that message. Otherwise, it is a nice little story.

Be a Cartoonist 60 min.

Random House Home Video/Imagination Tree

birth to 2 years	☒	5 to 11 years	☐	☐
2 to 5 years	☐	11 and older	☐	☐

In this "learning video" Alan Silberberg teaches children how to draw cartoons based on printed letters and numbers. It really works, and although the tape states it is for children eight and older, children a couple of years younger can do many of the pictures. The "kit" comes with drawing materials, so I doubt that you will find a rental version available. However, if you have some children who like to draw or color, this tape might well be worth buying.

Benji 87 min.

Vestron Video/Mulberry Square Productions

birth to 2 years	⊠	5 to 11 years	☐ ☐
2 to 5 years	☐	11 and older	☐ ☐

I always thought *Benji* was a Disney Productions film; it has that same warm feeling to it, and Benji has the same personality as his animated ancestor, Tramp, from *Lady and the Tramp*. But it is a production of Mulberry Square Productions, and a good one.

The story—which, for the uninitiated, is not animated—is about a young dog who lives very well by letting several families and friends care for him. But then Benji falls for a lovely lady dog, and his two favorite young "masters" are kidnaped. The movie resolves the adventure in a remarkably plausible way.

A nice tape—especially for dog lovers.

The Berenstain Bears' Comic Valentine 24 min.

Embassy Home Entertainment $9.95

birth to 2 years	☐	5 to 11 years	☐ ☐
2 to 5 years	☐ ☐	11 and older	☐

This Valentine's Day message from the Berenstain Bears is one of their nicer tapes. The plot centers around Brother's receiving several anonymous valentines from a Miss Honey Bear, and his subsequent attempts to find out her identity. The search is played out against the background of the upcoming championship hockey game against Brother's team's archrivals—the Beartown Bullies. Sister attempts to persuade her old friend Big Paw to attend the game, while Papa Bear once again bumbles about in an attempt to create the perfect Valentine for Mama Bear.

The best thing about this tape is that Miss Honey Bear does not turn out to be the cute cheerleader-type bear, but rather the mystery star goalie on the Beartown Bullies! She and Brother share a mutual love of hockey, and their relationship centers on helping to improve each other's game. A welcome change from the current video norms that hurry children into quasi-courting relationships before they even understand friendship.

The Berenstain Bears' Easter Surprise 25 min.

Embassy Home Entertainment/Nelson Entertainment $9.95	
birth to 2 years 📺	5 to 11 years 📺 📺
2 to 5 years 📺 📺	11 and older 📺

I liked the story line in this tape, which has some surprises. Basically, the story centers around the resignation of Boss Bunny—the Easter Bunny—who has, in essence, burned-out as a result of too much pressure and stress. The unique twist is that this resignation not only prevents Easter from coming, but Spring as well!

Brother and Papa Bear both take steps to remedy the situation. As usual, Papa fails while Brother's more innocent efforts succeed. Another plot twist, with an upside and a downside, features Sister Bear's birth, accompanied by the reappearance of Mama's lap and Brother's question, "Where do babies come from?" That is the upside—the tape provides parents with an opportunity to talk with their children about where babies come from. The downside is that the tape cops out with a chuckle and a segue to a song instead of answering Brother's question. Still, all in all, it is one of the better Berenstain Bear tapes.

The Berenstain Bears Meet Big Paw 24 min.

Embassy Home Entertainment/Nelson Entertainment $9.95	
birth to 2 years 📺	5 to 11 years 📺
2 to 5 years 📺	11 and older 📺

This Berenstain Bear story is their Thanksgiving message. And it is a good message about sharing and not being greedy. It does, however, stretch a little bit to make its point. For the most part, Bear Country is a pretty nice place to live—at least that is the impression we get from the other Berenstain Bear tapes. In this tape, however, all the Bears in Bear Country have become greedy, mean, food-hoarding Scrooges!

But such examples are useful in teaching us to be generous, kind, and helpful, which is what the cubs learn in this tape. Father, in his usual bumbling fashion, leads the town in fortifying itself against Big

Paw, who—legend says—will come and eat up the town should the Bears ever get greedy. And the town has become greedy, and a huge stranger has been seen in the Swamp. It all turns out fine, but this particular tape does not really hang together as well as most Berenstain Bear stories. It gets heavy on moral without much story to support it.

The Berenstain Bears Play Ball 24 min.

Embassy Home Entertainment/Nelson Entertainment $9.95

| birth to 2 years 📺 | 5 to 11 years 📺 📺 |
| 2 to 5 years 📺 📺 | 11 and older 📺 |

Again, if you overlook the lovable but dumb father figure, you have a good tape for kids. The story centers around baseball, pushy fathers, and talented girls. Father pushes Brother Bear into Little League with such fervor that Brother and his friends have to run off into the woods for a pick-up baseball game in order to play baseball for the fun of it. Father learns that the idea behind sports should be fun—not the vicarious fulfillment of Father's own lost dreams.

The other major plot line has to do with Father's overlooking Sister Bear's significant baseball talent, until everybody else has failed and Sister gets to show her stuff. There is a long musical number called "I Want It All" in which Sister states her intention to pilot jet airliners, have scads of children, wear high-fashion clothes, discover a cure for the common cold, cook and sew—"have her cake and eat it." In short, become a classic eighties Superwoman. The obvious message is that little girls should be allowed to explore traditionally male realms. For those liberated households out there who have been shocked to discover ultrafeminine tendencies lurking in the psyches of their four-, five- and six-year-old daughters, there is a more important message: Girls do too play baseball!

The Berenstain Bears' Christmas Tree 25 min.

Embassy Home Entertainment/Nelson Entertainment $14.95

| birth to 2 years 📺 | 5 to 11 years 📺 📺 |
| 2 to 5 years 📺 📺 | 11 and older 📺 📺 |

This tape reflects most of the qualities that have made these characters so popular. The tapes also teach good lessons. In this one Papa Bear takes the cubs off in search of the perfect Christmas tree, scorning the trees offered for sale in town. But they soon discover that every "good" tree for decorating is also someone's home. The cubs learn that you can't build your pleasure on someone else's misfortune.

But the tape also retains a recurring problem that has always afflicted the Berenstain Bears. Papa is—without doubt—stupid, which is not a terribly appealing message for us Papas who try to play a vital part in our children's upbringing. He has a good heart, is brave, and loves Mama and the cubs, but one wonders—as one did with Ozzie, on "Ozzie and Harriet"—how he ever manages to hold down a job that would pay for the family's bread and board. Would this distort children's perceptions of their fathers? Maybe not, but I make a point when watching Berenstain Bears with my children to talk about Papa's mental difficulties and say things like "Isn't it nice that Daddies aren't really that dumb? Mommy would have to do everything, wouldn't she?"

Calamity Jane 101 min.
_____

Warner Home Video

birth to 2 years ⊠	5 to 11 years □ □
2 to 5 years ⊠	11 and older □ □

I don't know if this is little girl specific or not, but my older daughter and her friends really like this tape. The music and action seem to suit them to a tee. It is the musical story of a grown-up tomboy (Doris Day) who eventually falls in love with and marries Wild Bill Hickok. While Native Americans do not fare very well in this 1950s musical, women do better than usual for films of this era. Calamity is never really "tamed"; she and Bill just come to realize that they like each other the way they are. I don't know if you will want to buy this tape, but put it up there close to the top of your rental list.

Challenge to Be Free 90 min.
_____

Media Home Entertainment

birth to 2 years ⊠	5 to 11 years □ □
2 to 5 years ⊠	11 and older □ □

Set in the far North, this adventure story is about "Trapper," a man whose love of animals triggers a series of events that turn him into a fugitive. The chase across the frozen North is exciting, and the ending will allow you to raise some interesting questions with your children about right and wrong. The tape is well done, with a good story line, wonderful photography, and a less-than-network level of violence. I would preview it for children under ten, but otherwise it is a good buy.

Race for Your Life, Charlie Brown 76 min.

Paramount Home Video

birth to 2 years ⊠	5 to 11 years ☐
2 to 5 years ☐	11 and older ⊠

A nice Peanuts adventure about the gang's exploits at camp. There are some good messages about competition and friendship. Still, I have some trouble recommending the tape very strongly because it offers nothing exceptional. Given the increasing quality and selection of children's tapes available, this one would not be very close to the top of my list.

It's Your First Kiss, Charlie Brown and Someday You'll Find Her, Charlie Brown 55 min.

Paramount Home Video

birth to 2 years ⊠	5 to 11 years ⊠
2 to 5 years ⊠	11 and older ⊠

It is somewhat unfair to call this a program-length commercial. "Peanuts" was a loved and insightful comic strip long before it was the marketing giant it is now. However, somewhere along the line Mr. Schultz was made aware that he had created a money-making machine. These two stories have nothing special to commend them, and were the "roles" not "played" by Peanuts characters the tape would never have been made. The quality of the stories does not improve just because the Peanuts gang presents them.

It's Magic, Charlie Brown and Charlie Brown's All-Stars 55 min.

Snoopy's Home Video Library

birth to 2 years ⊠	5 to 11 years ⊠
2 to 5 years ⊠	11 and older ⊠

This tape is another example of the negative impact of marketing potential on children's television. The Peanuts gang stars in two stories that would not have been made with other less marketable characters. No doubt the tapes will be rebroadcast, and no doubt many parents will see the Schultz name and buy the tapes. I do not suggest that you do the same.

Bon Voyage, Charlie Brown 76 min.

Paramount Home Video

| birth to 2 years | 🖾 | 5 to 11 years | 🖵 🖵 |
| 2 to 5 years | 🖵 | 11 and older | 🖵 |

Of the eleven Peanuts stories sent to me, this one is by far the best. It tells an interesting story in which the Peanuts gang goes to France as exchange students. There are elements of entertainment and mystery, and some good educational messages as well. If you feel compelled to have a Peanuts tape in your video library, this one is a good choice.

It's Flashbeagle, Charlie Brown and She's a Good Skate, Charlie Brown 60 min.

Media Home Entertainment

| birth to 2 years | 🖾 | 5 to 11 years | 🖵 |
| 2 to 5 years | 🖵 | 11 and older | 🖾 |

This tape contains two Peanuts specials. The first is *It's Flashbeagle, Charlie Brown*. I suppose that most cartoons are contrived, but one expects better from Charles Schultz. This one has no plot and is only occasionally amusing. It has the appearance of a set of daily Peanuts strips strung together with pointless songs.

The second story, *She's a Good Skate Charlie Brown*, is about Peppermint Patty's first figure-skating competition and fares much better than Flashbeagle. Although still disjointed, the story makes sense and is often amusing, and the music belongs with the rest of the story.

Play It Again, Charlie Brown 25 min.

Media Home Entertainment

| birth to 2 years | 🖾 | 5 to 11 years | 🖵 |
| 2 to 5 years | 🖵 | 11 and older | 🖾 |

Some of Charles Schultz's works are classics, but this particular tape is not one of them. It is essentially a series of cartoon strips animated and loosely hooked together by Schroeder playing his piano. The relationship, or rather the nonrelationship, between Lucy and Schroeder, which seems funny in small doses, gets a little oppressive in this longer version. Not the best model to put before the kids.

You're the Greatest, Charlie Brown and Life Is a Circus, Charlie Brown 60 min.

Media Home Entertainment/Snoopy's Home Video Library

| birth to 2 years | ☒ | 5 to 11 years | 📺 |
| 2 to 5 years | 📺 | 11 and older | ☒ |

Two half-hour specials appear on this tape. The first, *You're the Greatest, Charlie Brown*, is a pleasant story of Charlie Brown's attempt to win the decathlon at the local Junior Olympics. Charlie actually comes close, and in the process reflects on the value of working hard and doing your best.

The second story, *Life Is a Circus, Charlie Brown*, is proclaimed an Emmy winner on the tape box, but I did not find it as amusing as the first story. It is about Snoopy's exploits as a circus star in love with a performing poodle. The concept certainly limits the dialogue, and the story is predictable and bland.

Charlotte's Web 94 min.

Paramount Home Video

| birth to 2 years | 📺 📺 | 5 to 11 years | 📺 📺 📺 📺 |
| 2 to 5 years | 📺 📺 📺 | 11 and older | 📺 📺 📺 📺 |

Starting with one of the finest children's stories ever written gives this tape quite a head start on the competition. Still, I must admit that the folks who produced this animated version have held up their end of the bargain wonderfully well. *Charlotte's Web* is, of course, E. B. White's winsome tale of Wilbur the Pig who is saved from becoming bacon by the efforts of a wonderful spider named Charlotte. This story does what fine children's literature should do—while entertaining, it teaches the children about life, about friendship and death and miracles. The animation, narration, and music are all of the highest quality. If you only have room for one tape in your budget right now, and an audience between three and twelve years old, buy this tape.

Classic Fairy Tales: Vols. I, II and III 45–60 min.
___

Children's Video Library

birth to 2 years ☒   5 to 11 years ☒

2 to 5 years ☒   11 and older ☒

The boxes for these tapes talk about their being "ageless and time-less." In this instance that means old. These appear to be repackaged old cartoons from the early days of television; I remember seeing animation and sound of this style and quality in the mid-1950s, which was not the golden age of children's television. The box prices of $29.95–39.95 are further reason to pass on these particular offerings.

Don't Eat the Pictures 60 min.
___

Random House Home Video

birth to 2 years ☐   5 to 11 years ☐ ☐ ☐

2 to 5 years ☐ ☐ ☐   11 and older ☐

In this tape, subtitled *Sesame Street at the Metropolitan Museum of Art*, the characters from Sesame Street take us on a tour of the museum. Big Bird and Mr. Snuffleupagus get separated from the rest of the group, a snaf-upagus that causes the whole Sesame Street gang to get locked in the museum overnight. In a story line that ends very much like the Saint-Exupéry tale *The Little Prince*, Bird and Snuffy befriend a little Egyptian prince who is 4,706½ years old. In the meantime the rest of the Sesame Street gang scours the museum for Snuffy and Bird.

The story lines provide ample opportunity for the description and depiction of many of the museum's great artworks, as well as fostering a sense of wonder about museums and art in general. A very nice tape that seems to have a strong attraction for children as young as sixteen to eighteen months as well as the normal "Sesame Street" audience, which can run up into the lower elementary grades.

Draw and Color Far-Out Pets 60 min.
___

Playhouse Video

birth to 2 years ☒   5 to 11 years ☐ ☐ ☐

2 to 5 years ☐ ☐   11 and older ☐ ☐ ☐

In this "interactive video," Fred Lasswell, artist-writer of the syndi-cated cartoon strip Barney Google and Snuffy Smith, demonstrates how kids can draw cartoon versions of some animals and birds. A great alternative to "passive" viewing, the tape holds the attention of children as old as nine or ten but is simple enough to give even preschoolers a chance to duplicate some of the work.

Dr. Desoto 10 min.

Children's Circle Video

birth to 2 years ⊠	5 to 11 years ▢ ▢ ▢
2 to 5 years ▢ ▢	11 and older ▢ ▢

This tape, which is a direct video translation of the book by William Steig, is delightful. Like all the works by cc studios, it provides an easy transition between the video and the book, helping parents turn their young viewers into young readers. The story tells how Dr. Desoto, a dentist who happens to be a mouse, outsmarts a fox of a patient who intends to eat the Desotos with the new tooth the Doctor has provided. Desoto and his wife glue the fox's mouth shut under the pretext of painting his teeth with a miraculous new product that will prevent any further toothaches.

Note: Many of my Children's Circle Video stories come from "sampler" tapes. Each tape you purchase would contain a number of stories of various lengths.

Dumbo 63 min.

Walt Disney Home Video $29.95

birth to 2 years ▢	5 to 11 years ▢ ▢
2 to 5 years ▢ ▢	11 and older ▢ ▢

Children will love *Dumbo*, with the exception of the rather long drunken musical fantasy, which seems to bore them—and rightfully so. However, I cannot wholly endorse the film despite its winsome story, songs, and animation. It is, of course, the crows that are the problem. In the way they sing and dance, in the way they call each other "boy" and are called so by others as well, they are offensive caricatures of blacks. When my daughter saw the movie I explained to her that they were "characters, not like real people." And we talked about how—in the olden days—people used to make fun of other people because of how they looked or what color they were, and wasn't it nice that we didn't do that anymore. It is a talk worth having, because the rest of Dumbo's tale of how the little elephant with the big ears overcomes adversity to become a circus star is lovely.

The Edison Twins 75 min.

RCA/Columbia Pictures Home Video

birth to 2 years   ☒   5 to 11 years   ☐ ☐

2 to 5 years   ☐   11 and older   ☐ ☐

This series, which occasionally plays on the Disney Channel, reminds me of a modern "Spin and Marty," that old Walt Disney adventure series from the Mickey Mouse Club. The Edison twins are precocious kids who solve problems and meet challenges by virtue of superior intellectual ability. In the tape, which contains three episodes, the twins encounter a Northwoods "Windigo"—a Bigfootlike creature—while they participate in an orienteering contest. After winning the contest the kids stay on to investigate the Windigo, which turns out to be a mild-mannered salesman who is attempting to stop a questionable development on Lake Windigo. In each of the three episodes, the Edison twins solve a mini-mystery by applying some bit of scientific knowledge to the problems that confront them. Then at the end of each episode there is a little animated sequence that explains the scientific principle the children employed. These episodes are well done and would appeal to a wide age range.

The Emperor and the Nightingale 40 min.

Sony Video Software/Rabbit Ears Productions

birth to 2 years   ☒   5 to 11 years   ☐ ☐ ☐ ☐

2 to 5 years   ☐ ☐ ☐   11 and older   ☐ ☐ ☐

This tape is a fine example of the adaptation of children's literature to video. Glenn Close's narration and Mark Isham's music back lovely illustrations by Robert Van Nutt in this adaptation of Hans Christian Andersen's classic fairy tale. The story and the presentation are gentle and restful, which makes this a good tape for the "crazy hour," or any other time you want to help children calm down.

The tape is suitable for twos and threes who are used to being read to, but is interesting enough to hold the attention of much older children as well. It is a good tape, featuring Rabbit Ears Production's still-frame animation style in which camera movement and tightly edited still shots dominate.

Five Lionni Classics 30 min.

Random House Home Video

birth to 2 years ◻ ◻ ◻		5 to 11 years ◻
2 to 5 years ◻ ◻		11 and older ⊠

This tape contains five animal fables by Leo Lionni. There is the story of Frederick, the field mouse who collects sunrays, and Swimmy the fish, who teaches his friends to swim in a giant synchronized routine that makes them appear more frightening than their predators! These and the other tales are very well done. The animation is unique, having the appearance of torn or rough-cut paper figures, and there is a nice use of color and narration. We liked it a lot at our house.

Flash Cards: Multiplication, Division, Spell Well, Part 1 30 min. per tape

---

Child's Play Video

birth to 2 years ⊠		5 to 11 years ◻
2 to 5 years ◻		11 and older ◻

These tapes represent an interesting idea. They are, essentially, video flash cards. No frills, no animation, just—as the box says—a back-to-basics presentation of spelling and math drills. The tape is self-teaching so that learners can control the pace at which they work.

I do not have enough expertise in elementary education (the division and multiplication tapes I was sent are aimed at grades two through six) to suggest how, when, or if to use these tapes. But it is nice to know they are available, and if you feel a need in these areas you might want to check with your child's teacher about this product. The spelling tape, labeled Part 1, is designed for grade five through adult. Having just finished my college students' papers, spelling tapes for that audience seems like a good idea!

Five Stories for the Very Young 30 min.

Children's Circle Video

birth to 2 years ◻		5 to 11 years ⊠
2 to 5 years ◻ ◻		11 and older ⊠

This tape features five stories aimed at children from ages two to six. As usual the people at Children's Circle have selected only the highest quality children's books to translate into video, but these books take to that translation with varying degrees of comfort. "Harold's Fairy Tale," featuring Harold and his famous purple crayon, works wonderfully. Harold wanders through a kingdom he creates, drawing adventures until he gets tired and draws himself home. "Whistle for Willy" also works well as we follow young Willy through the trials of learning to whistle. "Caps for Sale" mixes monkeys and hats nicely. However, "Drummer Hoff" seems somewhat distant, and "Changes, Changes" works much better as a book that you read with a child sitting on your lap. But the last two stories suffer only in comparison with the other exceptional works on the tape. Taken as a whole, it is a very nice tape and worthy of your serious consideration.

Goldy: Last of the Golden Bears 90 min.

Vestron Video

birth to 2 years ⊠	5 to 11 years 📺 📺
2 to 5 years ⊠	11 and older 📺 📺

This amazingly plot-free movie is basically a series of very pretty nature scenes wrapped loosely around the story of a prospector and a little girl who befriend a young grizzly bear. In the course of the movie they lose each other, find gold, rescue Goldy (the bear) from an un-scrupulous circus owner, find each other, and eventually live happily ever after. It is a strange film; the acting is terribly simplistic and the situations are far more unrealistic than the most far-fetched sitcom, but there is something endearing about it. Perhaps it is just that good wins out over evil, no one is killed, and the locations in the Sequoia National Forest are beautiful. It is a great rental if available. For a purchase I would shop for a really good price.

Hans Brinker 103 min.

Warner Home Video

birth to 2 years ⊠	5 to 11 years 📺 📺
2 to 5 years ⊠	11 and older 📺 📺

An "oldie but a goody," this version of Mary Mapes Dodge's novel *Hans Brinker and the Silver Skates* is good entertainment for everyone in the family from about five on up. One of those rare tapes that can provide some nice entertainment for the whole family, it tells the story of a poor Dutch family who suffers through years of deprivation when the father is incapacitated in a construction accident. But they hang together and eventually triumph over adversity. A good tape.

Hans Christian Andersen 112 min.

Embassy Home Entertainment

birth to 2 years ⬚		5 to 11 years ⬚ ⬚ ⬚	
2 to 5 years ⬚ ⬚		11 and older ⬚ ⬚ ⬚	

This 1952 film is one that remains a classic, as they say, "for children of all ages." That means it is one of those tapes that parents can enjoy sitting through as well. Danny Kaye does a superb job in the title role as he helps to tell a wonderful fairy tale about the best fairy tale teller of them all.

There is plenty of music and dancing as we follow Hans to the enchanting city of Copenhagen and home again, learning about people, stories, love, and contentment. An excellent choice for everyone age three and older.

Heidi 105 min.

Vestron Video

birth to 2 years ⊠		5 to 11 years ⬚ ⬚ ⬚	
2 to 5 years ⬚ ⬚		11 and older ⬚ ⬚ ⬚	

This one is a classic. Originally aired in 1968 as a TV movie, this particular version stars Jennifer Edwards as Heidi and features Maximillian Schell, Jean Simmons, Sir Michael Redgrave, and Walter Slezak. Heidi is a young Swiss orphan who goes to live with her gruff old grandfather high in the Alps. What begins as the story of an unwelcome intrusion soon unfolds as a timeless lesson in love, courage, and strength. It's perfect for six-to-ten-year-old girls, and will get grudging attention and then genuine interest from most boys in the same age range.

Shop around for your best price, but this one is worth having.

Home Alone 30 min.

Hi-Tops Video $12.95

birth to 2 years ⊠		5 to 11 years ⬚ ⬚ ⬚	
2 to 5 years ⊠		11 and older ⬚ ⬚ ⬚	

This tape addresses the specific concerns of latchkey kids. The growing population of children who come home from school to an empty house do face some unique problems, and this tape addresses a lot of them: where to keep your key, how to answer the door or the phone, how best to spend your time, etc.

The tape is a touch simplistic; for example, it advocates using a spoon to spread peanut butter to avoid cutting yourself with a knife. However, the majority of the messages make sense and are helpful. If your kids fall into this category, or if you are the contact person for a latchkey kid, this tape is well worth the $12.95 price tag.

How Can I Tell If I'm Really in Love? 51 min.

Paramount Pictures

birth to 2 years	☒	5 to 11 years	☒
2 to 5 years	☒	11 and older	☐ ☐ ☐

This tape for teens is based on a number of books and concepts by Sol Gordon—whose name, you may have noticed, comes up in this book whenever kids, teens, love, and sex are mentioned. The narrators are Justine Bateman from "Family Ties," and Jason Bateman from "Valerie," with some help from Ted Danson of "Cheers." The real stars, however, are a bunch of teenagers from University High School in Los Angeles. There are a number of good things about this tape, aside from the excellent content. First, it reminds parents what it felt like to be a teenager. Second, it gives teenagers help in telling their parents what they are feeling. The content deals specifically with being "in love" and the relationship between "love," "sex," and "life." It is a very good tape that lets teens see sane messages about love and sex from the same medium that often provides them with the shallow and sleazy side of those issues.

The tape was directed and produced by Rick Hauser, who also wrote, produced, and directed *Strong Kids, Safe Kids.* His is not a high-profile job, but he really deserves a word of thanks for these projects he has undertaken to benefit our kids. Thanks, Rick!!

How the Rhinoceros Got His Skin and How the Camel Got His Hump 30 min.

Sony Video Software/Rabbit Ears Productions

birth to 2 years	☐	5 to 11 years	☐ ☐ ☐
2 to 5 years	☐ ☐ ☐	11 and older	☐ ☐

These two "Just So" stories by Rudyard Kipling should appeal to a wide range of children. Jack Nicholson's narration may be a little understated for preschoolers, but it is otherwise excellent and is accompanied by nice music from Bobby McFerrin. A good tape, employing still-frame animation, which shows the excellent illustrations to their best advantage.

Kids in Motion 66 min.

Playhouse Video

birth to 2 years 🖾		5 to 11 years 🖵 🖵
2 to 5 years 🖵 🖵		11 and older 🖵 🖵

This is a neat workout tape for kids. It combines music, poetry, dance, and games to get kids into a good workout. It's not a tape for all kids, but if Mom and Dad get huffing and puffing to their workout tapes, this is a nice, safe way to let the kids feel part of that aspect of the family.

Lady and the Tramp 75 min.

Buena Vista/Walt Disney Home Video $19.00–29.00

birth to 2 years 🖵		5 to 11 years 🖵 🖵 🖵 🖵
2 to 5 years 🖵 🖵 🖵 🖵		11 and older 🖵 🖵 🖵

This tape is touted on the box as being one of the "Classics." One learns to read videotape containers with a great degree of skepticism, but in this case that is not necessary. *Lady and the Tramp* really is a classic. The characters are charming, the music is delightful, and the animation is Disney at his best. The story seems to be one that children like to watch over and over. The message is definitely profamily, as the footloose Tramp settles down with Lady, accepts his license as a badge of responsibility, and becomes a proud Papa.

There are only two scenes that might frighten little ones. The first is a fight scene where Tramp rescues a fleeing Lady from a pack of mean dogs, and the other is the scene in which Lady and Tramp kill the rat in the baby's nursery. But they are both scenes that most children can be cuddled through, and shouldn't deter one from enjoying this delightful tape.

Learn 'n Play: Reading Volume #1—Journey to the Magic Jungle 30 min.

Scholastic-Lorimar

birth to 2 years ☒   5 to 11 years ▢

    2 to 5 years ▢   11 and older ☒

This tape combines a videotape, a Colorforms jungle playboard, plastic play pieces, and a tip sheet by a reading expert in an experience that is supposed to "promote reading readiness." However, it did not fare too well in our house. My daughter and her friends "did" it once, but then they contented themselves with sticking the pieces around the board and around the room while they watched other tapes. It might work much better in a structured setting, like a preschool or actually in the classroom. However, the tape is marketed with a home-use copyright that prohibits those applications.

The Lion, the Witch, and the Wardrobe 95 min.

Vestron Video

birth to 2 years ☒   5 to 11 years ▢ ▢

    2 to 5 years ☒   11 and older ▢ ▢

The Lion, the Witch, and the Wardrobe is an animated adaptation of a portion of C. S. Lewis's *Chronicles of Narnia*. It is billed as being presented by the Children's Television Workshop, and according to the tape jacket it won an Emmy for Outstanding Animated Program. It is a nice tape, but not among the best I have seen. The story is, of course, captivating, but the animation is stuck midway between the stylized still-frame animation of some of the narrated storybook tapes and the full animation of the Disney-type tapes. It takes a little getting used to, and it might be more problematic in another story. In this particular tape, however, one does get drawn into the tale of four human children who defeat the White Witch and, with the help of the regal Lion Aslan, ascend the thrones of the magic land of Narnia.

The Little Mermaid 26 min.

Random House Home Video

birth to 2 years ☒   5 to 11 years ▢ ▢

    2 to 5 years ▢   11 and older ▢

Richard Chamberlain narrates this adaptation of the well-known Hans Christian Andersen fairy tale. The tale of the Little Mermaid's ill-fated love for a human prince retains much of its charm. The animation is nicely done, and Chamberlain reads beautifully. However, some of my young advisers were less than pleased with the ending—more an assessment of the story than the tape.

My Little Pony 30 min.

Children's Video Library

birth to 2 years	⊠	5 to 11 years	⊠
2 to 5 years	⊠	11 and older	⊠

Although it is narrated by Sandy Duncan and Tony Randall, do not confuse this commercial with the animated storybooks narrated by other established stars. This particular tape links predatory flying dragons with an evil "Master" to put the Little Ponies in danger. Were the story more beguiling one might be tempted to overlook its obvious sales intent—but it isn't, so don't.

The Little Prince 88 min.

Paramount Home Video

birth to 2 years	⊠	5 to 11 years	▢
2 to 5 years	⊠	11 and older	▢

This movie is a strangely adult version of *The Little Prince*, and it is probably the least known of Lerner and Lowe's musicals. The original story by Antoine de Saint-Exupéry has always been a story that can be read at many levels. This film chooses to emphasize the most adult and poignant reading. It does it well, if unevenly, and is a good film for adults and teenagers. However, for children younger than that I cannot recommend it. The Little Prince's resurrection after dying from the snake's bite is a touch too subtle for most children. Hence, the last understandable image that the film leaves for them is the death of the Little Prince. It is not the ending intended and should not be the one given. I would suggest reading this excellent story to your young children, but if you must have a video version for them, choose another.

The Little Prince and Friends 90 min.

Pacific Arts Video

birth to 2 years ⊠	5 to 11 years ☐
2 to 5 years ⊠	11 and older ☐

This tape contains three "claymation" features. Claymation is a form of animation based on clay sculpting, and it is quite interesting in its own right. The three features are "The Little Prince," "Rip Van Winkle," and "Martin the Cobbler."

This version of "The Little Prince" is perhaps nicer for younger children than the feature film version. It is aimed at the seven- to ten-year-old audience, and the ending emphasizes the questions posed by the Little Prince's return to his planet—not his apparent death at the bite of the snake. The values from Saint-Exupéry's original tale—the power of love, the importance of the moment, and the wisdom of childhood—are all well preserved in this version.

"Rip Van Winkle" does not fair quite so well. Will Vinton, the creative force behind claymation, extends the story unnecessarily to provide more opportunity for his clay-based special effects. There is a dream sequence which, while technically interesting, might be frightening for the little ones. That is a shame, because the portions that remain true to the story are quite nice. "Martin the Cobbler" is probably not *all* that somber when you consider the fact that it is based on a story by Leo Tolstoy, who has never been known for light prose. And the story of the desolate old cobbler who rediscovers joy in his own life when he learns to live for others ends with a lightness that far outshines its darker beginnings. It is perhaps the best wedding of material and technique of the three stories. The claymation fits the earthy tones of Tolstoy's tale nicely.

The Adventures of the Little Prince 25 min.

Children's Video Library

birth to 2 years ⊠	5 to 11 years ☐ ☐
2 to 5 years ☐ ☐	11 and older ⊠

The episodes on this tape must be the initial episodes of the current broadcast series. The introduction to the tape states that the series is based on the character created by Antoine de Saint-Exupéry, and the episodes reflect many of the elements of the original story. However, the narrator also tells us that he is going to describe many of the Little

Prince's adventures in outer space. The series is somewhat like the "Care Bears" in its feel and is—at least in these two episodes—less simplistic and "action oriented" than some other morning cartoons that are available on video cassette. The tapes should not be confused with other actual adaptations of the Little Prince, but are pleasant tapes for preschool through first grade.

The Little Red Hen and the Three Billy Goats Gruff 30 min.

Scholastic-Lorimar/Blue Ribbon Storybook

birth to 2 years	📺	5 to 11 years	📺
2 to 5 years	📺 📺	11 and older	☒

   Each story in this tape has essentially two sections. The first section is an animated adaptation of the old folktales. The Little Red Hen's message about work, responsibility, and reward comes through nicely. The message is accentuated in the second section when the Little Red Hen, in puppet form, chats with the viewer about the story and its meaning.

   The Three Billy Goats Gruff does not work as well. The animated story is nice, the artwork pleasant, and the Billy Goat's song engaging. However, the puppet-talk session gets a little strained. The Troll puppet—our host for this section—confesses to the audience that he has a problem. But it turns out that his problem is greed; with nary a word about leaving the goats alone, he regrets not having eaten the first goat. Although created for three- to eight-year-olds, best for the younger end of that scale; six-year-olds and up will find it slow and somewhat simplistic.

Mickey's Christmas Carol 30 min.

Buena Vista Home Video $14.95

birth to 2 years	📺	5 to 11 years	📺 📺
2 to 5 years	📺 📺	11 and older	📺 📺

   This tape is really a very nice animated version of Dickens's classic *Christmas Carol*. With Uncle Scrooge as Scrooge and Mickey as Bob Cratchit, it serves as a good introduction to the story for young children, who might still be scared by the more adult versions starring George C. Scott or Henry Winkler.

More Baby Songs 30 min.

Hi-Tops Video

birth to 2 years ☐ ☐		5 to 11 years ☐
2 to 5 years ☐ ☐		11 and older ☒

The box tells me that this tape is "following on the heels of the original hit *Baby Songs*." I have not seen that tape, but if it is like this one you might want to give each of them a look. These music videos for the preschool set are genuinely fun. The music is bouncy and the accompanying video nice. When my youngest was about 18 months old she really enjoyed the baby chimp featured in "Sittin' in a High Chair."

Mowgli's Brothers 30 min.

Family Home Entertainment

birth to 2 years ☒		5 to 11 years ☐ ☐
2 to 5 years ☐ ☐		11 and older ☐ ☐

This tape is an animated adaptation of a story from Rudyard Kipling's *The Jungle Book*. I liked it a great deal, and so did most of the kids I showed it to in the age range the tape suggests, three to eight years. The animation and narration are both well done. The story of Mowgli's growing up among the wolves, and gaining the friendship of the bear and the leopard and the enmity of Shere Khan the tiger, has entertained generations of children. This tape continues that tradition and will not detract from a child's appreciation of the written work.

Oliver Twist 72 min.

Vestron Video

birth to 2 years ☒		5 to 11 years ☐ ☐
2 to 5 years ☐		11 and older ☐ ☐

This tape is another good animated version of the Dickens classic. My six-year-old found it quite entertaining, and it would probably stretch to children several years older as well. It is part of something called "The Charles Dickens Collection," which the cover touts as "a unique home video collection of literary master-pieces." While the tapes should certainly not substitute for the original novels for adolescents, the series seems to be a nice way to introduce children to the stories and characters.

Panama 12 min.

Children's Circle Video

birth to 2 years ☐ ☐   5 to 11 years ☐ ☐

  2 to 5 years ☐ ☐ ☐   11 and older ☒

This tape tells a delightful story about a little bear and a little tiger who set off to find "Panama, the land of our dreams!" Their trip is circular rather than wide-ranging, eventually returning them to their own doorstep. Their house shows more promise, the trees and shrubs are larger and grander than before—certainly this is "Panama, land of our dreams!"

As with all Children's Circle Video tapes, the illustrations mirror the original book, *The Trip to Panama* by Janosch.

The Patient Ramona 23 min.

Lorimar Home Video

birth to 2 years ☒   5 to 11 years ☐ ☐ ☐

  2 to 5 years ☐   11 and older ☐ ☐ ☐

Beverly Cleary is one of the great children's story tellers. This series, which is currently running on my local PBS station, is a fairly faithful version of the Ramona books. This episode is a delightful study of a child's getting sick and staying home from school, putting together a book report, etc. It offers no super heroes or chase scenes, nor is it great and enduring literature. But it does offer a winsome look at "everyday." It is an especially good tape for sick kids; I happened to review it when both my girls were down with the chicken pox. Talk about art imitating life!

Pee-Wee's Big Adventure 92 min.

Warner Home Video

birth to 2 years ☒   5 to 11 years ☒

  2 to 5 years ☒   11 and older ☐ ☐

"Pee-Wee's Playhouse," the television show, is strange, but it is all funny strange. *Pee-Wee's Big Adventure* has tossed in enough material for adults to push it fairly far down the list for younger kids. The ghost ride on the truck and some of the dream sequences rule it out for those six and under. The sexual innuendo will probably get a laugh from the junior high schoolers, but it is pretty cheap humor. This is one of those instances where—at least for most audiences—the TV series is far better than the film.

The Popples: A Clean Sweep 29 min.

RCA/Columbia Pictures Home Video

birth to 2 years ☒	5 to 11 years ☒
2 to 5 years ☒	11 and older ☒

This program-length commercial is foolish even by Saturday morning standards. The plot centers around the toys by the same name, which clean a kid's room while he—what else—watches television! Actually, "plot" is an exaggeration; the action in this tape shifts from one locale to another with no discernible shift in dialogue or action. The dialogue is all pun-based one-liners that do nothing to create or advance a story. The action is all Popples or the kids running, jumping, pointing, or laughing—again with no discernible story line. I do not know whether the tape I was sent was one episode or two, but it really makes no difference. I would advise against renting or purchasing the tape regardless of length or cost.

Ramona's Rainy Day 24 min.

Lorimar Home Video

birth to 2 years ☒	5 to 11 years ☐ ☐ ☐
2 to 5 years ☐	11 and older ☐ ☐ ☐

Another Ramona tape. This time the rain spoils a planned trip to the fair, leaving the family trapped with one another and the Sunday blahs. Ramona drives everyone nuts wanting them to play with her. Everyone gets on everyone else's nerves, and chaos rules. I am not really sure what makes these particular tapes so endearing; perhaps it is because they are such nonfiction fiction. Ms. Cleary has definitely been lurking around our house on occasion stealing material for her books and the subsequent tapes.

Rapunzel 45 min.

CBS/Fox Children's Video/Playhouse Video $19.98

birth to 2 years ☒	5 to 11 years ☐ ☐
2 to 5 years ☒	11 and older ☐ ☐

This tape is one of a series that make up Faerie Tale Theatre—apparently a project of Shelley Duvall, who stars in the title role of *Rapunzel*. It is a nicely done tape, with the type of broad characterizations, effects, and sets usually found in children's theater.

I would not suggest it for children any younger than five years old, but it will probably be well received by the six- to nine-year-old crowd.

Reading Rainbow 60 min.

Children's Video Library

birth to 2 years ⊠	5 to 11 years ☐ ☐ ☐	
2 to 5 years ☐ ☐	11 and older ☐ ☐	

The Children's Video Library sent a number of tapes from the "Reading Rainbow" series—with good reason. Hosted by LeVar Burton, and still being aired by Public Television, "Reading Rainbow" presents video versions of quality children's books using original illustrations and skillful readers to make the selected works come alive. The program also features book reviews by young readers that coax viewers to check the books out of their local libraries and read them. The Children's Video Library packages two of the half-hour programs on each tape, which is helpful for those who cannot get the program locally or who want to fill in gaps in their own "Reading Rainbow" off-air-recordings.

The level of the program shifts a bit depending upon the book selected, but I would certainly encourage you to share it with your "pre-readers" as well as with your young readers.

The Red Balloon 34 min.

Embassy Home Entertainment/Nelson Entertainment $14.95

birth to 2 years ⊠	5 to 11 years ☐ ☐	
2 to 5 years ☐	11 and older ☐ ☐	

I would definitely recommend this fascinating tape of the critically acclaimed film. It is a story about a boy and a balloon, a wondrous red balloon that follows the boy everywhere and proves to be a true and devoted friend.

The aspect of the tape that I find most intriguing is its indefinability. I have seen it more than a few times and still do not know whether it is a child's film about a balloon, or an adult film about childhood. Maybe it does not matter. Either way, it is a winsome piece.

Rikki-Tikki-Tavi 30 min.

Family Home Entertainment

birth to 2 years ☒		5 to 11 years ☐ ☐
2 to 5 years ☐ ☐		11 and older ☐ ☐

This adaptation of a story from Rudyard Kipling's *The Jungle Book* has the added attraction of being narrated by Orson Welles. His wonderful voice provides an excellent background for nicely done animation.

Rikki-Tikki-Tavi is the time-honored story of a mongoose and his battle with two evil cobras, Nag and Nagaina. The snakes are nasty, and I would not suggest letting any preschool- or kindergarten-aged kids watch it without some parental cuddling available close at hand. However, the actual fight scenes between Rikki and the snakes are done rather obliquely with long shots that are slightly off-camera and out of sight down the cobra's hole, etc. As such they provide a good transition between the conflict-free tapes that are best suited for two-, three-, and four-year-olds, and the more graphic "fight scenes" that they will inevitably encounter—and for which they should be prepared. The box suggests a three to eight age range, which seems appropriate.

Rosie's Walk 4 min.

Children's Circle Video

birth to 2 years ☐ ☐		5 to 11 years ☐
2 to 5 years ☐ ☐		11 and older ☒

Another typical Children's Circle tape that faithfully translates good books into good video. Nice narration and a bouncy sound track keep this adaptation of Pat Hutchins's book moving right along. It is the story of a chicken named Rosie who takes a stroll around the farmyard, closely followed by the world's most unfortunate fox.

Rumpelstiltskin 84 min.

Media Home Entertainment

birth to 2 years ☒		5 to 11 years ☐ ☐
2 to 5 years ☐		11 and older ☐ ☐

Amy Irving is the miller's daughter and Billy Barty stars in the title role of this version of the old fairy tale in which a young girl trades the rights to her firstborn to a gnome in exchange for the ability to spin straw into gold. When the child is born, however, the young mother realizes she cannot give the child up and begs the gnome for a reprieve. He says that she may keep the child only if she can guess his name. Well, you know the rest—or if you do not I will not spoil it for you.

This tape definitely makes a good week-end rental, and may be a good buy for the right price.

Sesame Street: Play Along Games and Songs 30 min.

Random House Home Video/Sesame Street Home Video

birth to 2 years	☐	5 to 11 years	☐ ☐
2 to 5 years	☐ ☐	11 and older	☐

This tape is a compilation of games and songs from the PBS series with some new bits added. It is of the same high quality as the broadcast program and comes with a little workbook. I do not rate it as highly as the program simply because one of the wonderful features of the Sesame Street program is that it is free, and the tape is not.

Sleeping Beauty 74 min.

Walt Disney Home Video

birth to 2 years	☐	5 to 11 years	☐ ☐ ☐ ☐
2 to 5 years	☐ ☐ ☐	11 and older	☐ ☐ ☐ ☐

Undoubtedly one of Disney's best works for children—perhaps his very best—this telling of the timeless fairy tale of how good conquers evil for true love's sake manages as much impact as any of its high-tech descendants such as *Star Wars*. It demonstrates why Disney's blending of music and animation remains the standard against which all others are judged. The final climactic fight scene with the dragon may require some cuddling of those five and under, but it passes rather quickly and is mild compared to some normal Saturday morning cartoons.

Smile for Auntie 6 min.

Children's Circle Video

birth to 2 years ☐		5 to 11 years ☐ ☐	
2 to 5 years ☐ ☐		11 and older ☐ ☐	

I do not know if children will find this tape too terribly amusing, but it will tickle the funny bone of any parent who suffers through friends' and relatives' attempts to get a smile out of the baby. As in the other tapes by Children's Circle reviewed here, the treatment is faithful to the original, in this case a book by Diane Paterson.

Strong Kids, Safe Kids 45 min.

Paramount Home Video

birth to 2 years ☒		5 to 11 years ☐ ☐ ☐ ☐	
2 to 5 years ☐ ☐		11 and older ☐ ☐ ☐ ☐	

This very interesting tape deals specifically with preventing sexual abuse of children, and generally with establishing open and honest communication between adults and children. It is a frank and—from the perspective of our family—wonderful tape. But it is a tape that parents should preview before sharing with their children. This warning is more for the benefit of the parents than the kids. There is nothing on this tape that is inappropriate for parents to discuss with their children. But if you are like me you will do a better job if you have a little time to think things out first. The tape presents Henry Winkler and his alter ego, the Fonz, as narrators. It also features some other Hollywood types, live and animated, as well as some excellent sessions with Sol Gordon, whose books I have recommended earlier, and Kee MacFarlane from the Children's Institute International. This tape is an important one for families with children of all ages.

The Tale of Mr. Jeremy Fisher and the Tale of Peter Rabbit 30 min.

Sony Video Software/Rabbit Ears Productions

birth to 2 years ☐ ☐ ☐		5 to 11 years ☐ ☐ ☐	
2 to 5 years ☐ ☐ ☐ ☐		11 and older ☐ ☐	

Meryl Streep does the narration on these two tales by Beatrix Potter. As is also the case with the other Rabbit Ears Productions reviewed, this tape features original music and still-frame animations. This animation style presents the original watercolors quite effectively, giving the tapes their quiet but interesting signature. The illustrations and music of the three tapes from this studio were of uniformly high quality.

The Beatrix Potter stories have delighted us for generations and these renditions continue in that proud tradition. We all enjoyed them, including the baby, who seemed genuinely interested in the music and shifting colors.

Tales of Beatrix Potter 43 min.

Children's Video Library

birth to 2 years	□ □		5 to 11 years	□ □ □
2 to 5 years	□ □ □		11 and older	□ □

This tape contains a wide-ranging collection of old Beatrix Potter favorites. Peter Rabbit, Benjamin Bunny, Miss Moppet, Tom Kitten, and the Two Bad Mice are all included along with a "read-along session" of Cecily Parsley's nursery rhymes. Penny Yrigoyen's illustrations are charming. Sydney S. Walker does a good job telling the stories in a gentle tone that makes this an exceptionally nice quiet-time tape.

While Potter's works appeal to all ages, this tape seems to play best to children from about four to seven or eight years old.

Teddy Ruxpin: Guest of the Grunges 35 min.

Hi-Tops Video

birth to 2 years	⊠		5 to 11 years	⊠
2 to 5 years	⊠		11 and older	⊠

This tape is essentially a program-length commercial aimed at hyping Teddy Ruxpin products. The story and characters offer nothing different from normal Saturday morning commercial fare, and although the tape wraps up with a brief chat from a big Teddy Ruxpin puppet-person about making cookies for your friends, I certainly would not recommend spending money for it. I would not even recommend it for free viewing on commercial broadcast. It is just a bland time-filler.

The Three Robbers 5 min.

Children's Circle Video

birth to 2 years ☐

2 to 5 years ☐ ☐ ☐

5 to 11 years ☐ ☐ ☐

11 and older ☐

The spoken and sung sound effects add a delightful flavor to this rendition of Tomi Ungerer's tale of three highwaymen who adopt, house, and care for an entire town of lost, abandoned, or unhappy children. The animation retains the enchanting feel of Ungerer's original illustrations.

Vanishing Wilderness 90 min.

Media Home Entertainment

birth to 2 years ☒

2 to 5 years ☐

5 to 11 years ☒

11 and older ☒

The tape box carries the following quote from former President Reagan: "Sheer beauty is the only way to describe 'Vanishing Wilderness.'" There are some beautiful sequences in the tape, and adults—especially busy adults doing something else—might well overlook the many disjointed and boring sections. My young viewers were not willing to give it that much leeway. There is no discernible story line to hold the photography together, and the narration falls well below the information level that young PBS nature program viewers will expect. President Reagan probably got his copy as a gift. If you can get one that way fine; otherwise give this one a pass.

The Velveteen Rabbit 25 min.

Random House Home Video/Rabbit Ears Productions

birth to 2 years ☐ ☐

2 to 5 years ☐ ☐ ☐ ☐

5 to 11 years ☐ ☐ ☐ ☐

11 and older ☐ ☐ ☐ ☐

This tape is another excellent example of the high-quality product that can result from combining the best elements. Margery Williams's story has been loved for so long, and by so many generations of children and parents, that it—like the rabbit it chronicles—must have become real. The tape employs the still-frame animation of all the Rabbit Ears Productions tapes, and the process does full justice to David Jorgensen's illustrations. Meryl Streep's narration is mesmerizing and magical. All in all, a delightful experience that carries a wonderful message of love and caring, of patience and reward.

Watership Down 90 min.

Warner Home Video

| birth to 2 years | ⊠ | 5 to 11 years | ☐ |
| 2 to 5 years | ⊠ | 11 and older | ☐ ☐ ☐ ☐ |

This animated version of Richard Adams's novel tells the story of a group of rabbits who flee the destruction of their home and wander in search of the ideal place to establish a better life. The tape explores religion, social justice, friendship, and power as the rabbits seek their better world. It is extremely well done, but you need to take the PG rating seriously: it means parental guidance, and the film is definitely *not* for children under ten. There are some very realistic fight scenes and some genuinely unsettling nightmare scenes.

Given that proviso, let me emphasize that this is a marvelous tape, with excellent animation, good narration, and fine music.

What about Love, Mister Rogers? 51 min.

Playhouse Video

| birth to 2 years | ⊠ | 5 to 11 years | ☐ ☐ ☐ |
| 2 to 5 years | ☐ ☐ ☐ | 11 and older | ☐ ☐ |

Two episodes of the PBS series "Mister Rogers' Neighborhood" are packaged on how even people who love one another very much can get very angry with one another. Like most of Mr. Rogers's shows they are well done and very insightful. The concern is obviously whether one wants to spend money for a program that is still available on PBS. If you have no access to Mr. Rogers on PBS, or if your reception is poor enough to prohibit off-the-air taping, then you might want to purchase this tape. Otherwise I would stand by my earlier strong recommendation of the program and would advise having my own homemade Mr. Rogers tape close at hand.

The White Seal 30 min.

Family Home Entertainment

| birth to 2 years | ☐ | 5 to 11 years | ☐ ☐ |
| 2 to 5 years | ☐ ☐ | 11 and older | ☐ ☐ |

Family Home Entertainment continues its tradition of using first-quality narrators for its animated versions of stories from *The Jungle Book* by Rudyard Kipling. Roddy McDowall does the narration for this less-well-known tale of a young white seal in search of a safe haven for his family and friends.

This is another well done and entertaining tape for three- to eight-year-olds. The younger ones will need some cuddling during their first exposure to the hunt scene. But the violence is mostly implied, as it is in all the *Jungle Book* tapes I saw from this producer. It is a good piece of work.

Wizards of the Lost Kingdom 76 min.

Media Home Entertainment

birth to 2 years ☒	5 to 11 years ☒
2 to 5 years ☒	11 and older ☐

According to my eight- to ten-year-old experts, there is not really much to get excited about in this film, and I am afraid I concur. It is a decent time-filler, but that rarely qualifies a tape for inclusion in our library.

Essentially it is the story of a young wizard who must battle an evil sorcerer for control of the kingdom. There are some laser-type special effects, but nothing really new or interesting. Finally, as the father of two daughters, the generally sexist tone bothers me. Just because they are in a kingdom does not mean that the girls and women have to appear in frilly, lacy semi-nightgowns, nor does it mean that they cannot do anything more interesting than suffer with strength.

Wonder of It All 94 min.

Media Home Entertainment

birth to 2 years ☒	5 to 11 years ☐
2 to 5 years ☒	11 and older ☐

This tape is produced by Pacific International Enterprises, which also produced the Wilderness Family tapes. This particular tape—like *Vanishing Wilderness*, also produced by this company—suffers from the lack of both a connected story line and a clear educational objective. In the Wilderness Family tapes the lengthy nature footage retains children's attention because it contributes to, or is at least contained in, a story. I give this tape a higher rating than *Vanishing Wilderness* because the more varied visuals seemed to hold the children's attention better.

The Wonderful Wizard of Oz 93 min.

RCA/Columbia Pictures Home Video

birth to 2 years 📺		5 to 11 years 📺 📺
2 to 5 years 📺 📺		11 and older 📺 📺

This animated version of the old tale is certainly not Judy Garland and Company, or even *The Wiz*. However, it has the benefit of being less frightening for preschoolers, and I do not think I have seen any of the characters on sale in any toy store. The animation seems to be by the same people who did "Belle and Sebastian" for Nickelodeon; as a matter of fact there is a striking resemblance between Sebastian and Dorothy! It is a good rental choice if available, and it might qualify as a purchase.

Zoobilee Zoo 22 min. per episode

RCA/Columbia Pictures Home Video

birth to 2 years ⊠		5 to 11 years 📺
2 to 5 years 📺		11 and older ⊠

The tape provides three episodes of this program-length commercial. The shows focus on moral issues faced by the Zoobles, humans made up to look like various animals. The fact that the episodes do attempt to teach laudable values—truth, kindness, etc.—makes them preferable to the other program-length commercials that merely market mayhem. But the show just never seems to get going.

The make up and costumes, however, are wonderful. My older daughter is fascinated by them, although her younger sister finds some of them scary. Since my local PBS station has opted to carry the program I am glad the dolls have not been a success; none of the Hallmark Stores here (Zoobles are a Hallmark creation and they sponsor the show) carries them anymore. I hope they do not resurface in conjunction with this new PBS release.

Broadcast Programs

I should make a disclaimer as I begin to deal with those programs that appear on our television screens via the airwaves or our cable systems. There is an overload of material out there, and it comes and goes with remarkable rapidity. The information I provide in these sections tends to fall into two categories: first, programs we have enjoyed and think you might, too; second, programs I have been asked about with some degree of frequency. I make no pretense of dealing with everything out there that has merit. My suggestions are just a good place to start.

The Public Broadcasting System (listed as PBS or CPT in *TV Guide* and other listings) is still the best source of broadcast programming for children, largely because it remains the home of "Sesame Street," which is clearly the best program available for infants to preschoolers. Ratings and descriptions for this and other broadcast programs follow.

"Sesame Street"

birth to 2 years ☐ ☐ ☐ ☐		5 to 11 years ☐ ☐ ☐
2 to 5 years ☐ ☐ ☐ ☐		11 and older ☒

This program does so many things well. It was originally designed to provide inner-city children with the preschool experience many of them were missing. According to the kindergarten teachers I have talked with it does that for *everyone*. They claim to be able to distinguish readily between "Street Watchers" and "Non-Street Watchers." Those who watch, they tell me, are significantly ahead in the basics of color and shape recognition, alphabet skills, and general reading readiness.

Those opinions certainly parallel my own perceptions. Both of our girls began to watch "Street" very early, and it was a great preschool experience for them.

"Mister Rogers' Neighborhood"

birth to 2 years ☐ ☐ ☐ ☐		5 to 11 years ☐ ☐ ☐
2 to 5 years ☐ ☐ ☐ ☐		11 and older ☒

This PBS program runs a close second to "Sesame Street" as the program I would choose for my preschoolers and early-elementary-school-age children if I had to give them only one program. As I have said earlier in the book, Fred Rogers is the ideal big smiley face. His program provides wonderful lessons about self-confidence, cooperation, sharing, and other values. With its neighborhood of Make-Believe, it is also the ideal program to teach the Golden Rule of Television that real and make-believe are different.

Finally, and this is very important, it is one program that presents little boys with a gentle role model. Women have long pointed out the stereotypical images of women that television presents to little girls. The same is true for little boys, who are beset on every side with men who shoot, hit, seduce, smoke, and drink their way through life. Fred Rogers provides a welcome respite from that barrage.

"Jim Henson's Muppet Babies"

| birth to 2 years ☒ | 5 to 11 years 📺 📺 📺 📺 |
| 2 to 5 years 📺 📺 📺 | 11 and older 📺 📺 |

For my money this NBC Saturday morning offering is the best commercial network program around for the younger set. I have seen children as old as eight or nine watch it when they thought no one was looking. It is a wonderfully creative program, both in its conception and in its execution. Its mix of animation, film, and print not only heightens the impact of the program, but also demonstrates to the kids that television is "make believe, not real." And who can object to a program that helps teach one of the Golden Rules of Television?

"Square One TV"

| birth to 2 years ☒ | 5 to 11 years 📺 📺 📺 📺 |
| 2 to 5 years 📺 📺 | 11 and older 📺 📺 📺 📺 |

This PBS program takes the teaching of math into a world I wish I had known when I was in elementary school. A number of delightful and entertaining features make this program a valuable learning experience for kids in grades one through five, with some overlap on each end.

"Wonderworks"

| birth to 2 years ☒ | 5 to 11 years 📺 📺 |
| 2 to 5 years ☒ | 11 and older 📺 📺 📺 📺 |

This series on PBS airs a variety of programs, but the quality is almost always exceptional. The programs usually deal with important issues and are most often aimed at children ten and over. Unless you are a regular viewer I would suggest that you tape them first, preview them, and then view them with your children if you feel they are appropriate.

"ABC After-School Specials"

birth to 2 years ☒	5 to 11 years ☐ ☐ ☐
2 to 5 years ☐	11 and older ☐ ☐ ☐

This is an anthology like "Wonderworks," but it has a number of programs that appeal to a younger audience. It is one of preciously few sources of good children's programming on the networks these days. Watch your program guide, or call the programming director of your local ABC affiliate for an idea of what is coming up.

"Cosby"

birth to 2 years ☒	5 to 11 years ☐ ☐ ☐
2 to 5 years ☐ ☐	11 and older ☐ ☐ ☐

I think you will find this series a genuine delight to share with your family, especially if you shop around through the syndicated versions until you find the episodes that overlap most closely with the ages and concerns of your own children. In our market you can get three different "seasons" of "Cosby," two in syndicated reruns with younger Cosby kids, and, of course, the current episodes.

Some of the best programs out there for children are episodes of programs that are designed for adults. PBS offers "Nova," "Wild America," "Wild, Wild World of Animals," "National Geographic Specials," "The Voyage of the Mimi," and a host of other series, all of which offer episodes that will educate and enchant your children.

I must say, truthfully, that nothing else comes to mind. There may well be other good things out there, but those mentioned above *more* than fill up our allotted time for television!

Cable Programs

As I mentioned earlier, your selection of cable programs depends upon the cable system to which you subscribe. The various stations make a wide variety of programming available. There are three cable networks in particular that increase your options for children. They are Nickelodeon, The Disney Channel, and CBN.

Nickelodeon bills itself as a channel just for children, and it is. Although not all of its programs are ones I would select, the following are exceptional:

"Today's Special"

birth to 2 years ☐ ☐	5 to 11 years ☐ ☐ ☐
2 to 5 years ☐ ☐ ☐ ☐	11 and older ☒

This program, which rivaled "Sesame Street" for a few years in our house, is about a mannequin named Jeff who magically comes to life at night. He and Jody, the young woman in charge of creating the displays that promote "today's special" in the department store, weave some excellent messages into a nice blend of story and song. They are assisted by Muffy the mouse and Sam the night watchman. The interracial, mixed-age cast addresses a wide variety of issues and concerns that enthralled our girls in their preschool years. This Canadian import is well worth keeping; one only wishes we could have a few more episodes. A special note on this program: a number of PBS affiliates now carry it, making it available to noncable viewers.

"The Elephant Show with Sharon, Lois, and Braham"

birth to 2 years ☐ ☐ ☐	5 to 11 years ☐ ☐ ☐
2 to 5 years ☐ ☐ ☐ ☐	11 and older ☐

This Nickelodeon show is a delightful music show for the little ones. It begins to appeal to children at the age of about one, and still gets good reviews from six- and seven-year-olds.

The Disney Channel, as I mentioned in the chapter on shopping for cable systems, is a premium channel. The quality of programs is more even than on Nickelodeon, but they still bear monitoring.

"The Wind in the Willows"

birth to 2 years ☐ ☐ ☐	5 to 11 years ☐ ☐
2 to 5 years ☐ ☐ ☐	11 and older ☒

"Welcome to Pooh Corner"

birth to 2 years ☐	5 to 11 years ☐ ☐ ☐
2 to 5 years ☐ ☐ ☐	11 and older ☐ ☐

The two series that we enjoyed most. They are both based on the novels contained in the titles, and they are nice tastes of each. "Walt Disney Presents" has some nostalgic value for people who grew up with it, but it is beginning to show its age badly in spots. The Disney Channel is perhaps most noteworthy for its selection of family movies and occasional specials.

CBN, which used to be the Christian Broadcasting Network although I don't see it listed that way any longer, is worth looking into because it has picked up all those old domestic comedies and other "family fare" from the fifties and sixties. Some of them seem silly now, but others have aged well.

TBS, the Turner Broadcasting System, is not really an afterthought, but much of its programming is duplicated elsewhere in this chapter. That obviously makes it a good option when you are shopping for a cable system. However, I include it here at the end of the cable selections because it is our sole source for an excellent program.

"National Geographic Explorer"

birth to 2 years ⊠	5 to 11 years □ □ □
2 to 5 years □	11 and older □ □ □

This two-hour-long program is a young people's look at many of the fascinating people, places, and things explored by the works of the National Geographic Society. The length of the program can be a problem, but one that can be overcome by taping and dividing the program into segments around dinner, homework, yardwork, etc.

The information in this chapter is by no means all-inclusive. Let me know what I have missed, and I will include it in the next edition. But the point is that there are some good "tomorrow's memories" out there in the video bookstore. We just need to shop a little more wisely. Good luck.

Appendix: The Media Probe

This particular version of the Media Probe is a little more advanced than the one in Chapter 4. However, it is based on the same premises and has the same objective. Before using this version you might want to review that portion of the chapter.

Plotting the Action

Media Probe Premise 1 states that all television programs follow a dramatic structure. We can sketch out that dramatic structure by turning a regular 8½-by-11-inch sheet of paper on its side and dividing it into four columns with the following labels: "Normal," "Rising Action," "Climax," "Resolution."

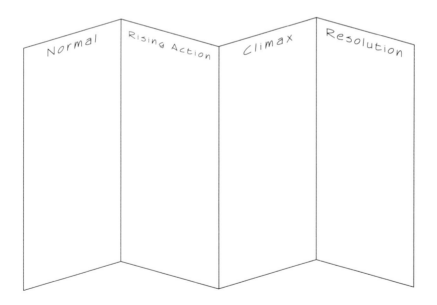

Normal

In this column we jot down what we understand to be the normal state of affairs in the program. Since any example I use will be dated anyway, let's go back to one of my favorite examples—the "Family Ties" episode in which Alex meets his first college sweetheart, Ellen. In column one for "Family Ties" we might write something like this: "Show deals with family exploring its 'ties' to each other and other people. Parents are aging former hippies who are now part of the mainstream. Oldest son (Alex) is conservative and arrogant but insecure. Oldest daughter (Mallory) is usually seen as a preppie, air-head type but occasionally shows some good insight. Younger daughter (Jennifer) is a bit of a jock, having some trouble adjusting. Andy is the baby of the family, idolizes older brother, does cute things."

This entry in the "Normal" column tells us what the situation of the program is and prepares us to fill in the next column, "Rising Action," which charts the unfolding plot line.

Rising Action

As we mentioned in Premise 1, all television programs follow the basics of dramatic structure. The normal state we just defined is disturbed by the introduction of conflict—somebody rocks the boat, forcing the action that creates the story. In this column we include those action elements. Sticking with the "Family Ties" example we might jot down the following in the "Rising Action" column:

1. Alex meets Ellen, his girlfriend's roommate.
2. They don't agree about anything, but end up getting thrown together in a lot of different situations.
3. They end up at a dance together, they kiss, Ellen runs off.
4. Ellen decides to marry old boyfriend. Alex gets depressed.
5. Alex drives Ellen to train so she can go get married. They fight.
6. Alex goes home, talks to Mom about Ellen, leaves for Economics Department banquet.

These notes are not intended to describe *everything* that went on in the program, but rather to help us recall what happened when we come back to go through the rest of the steps of the Media Probe. In this column the action steps are the ones that take us up to the next column, "Climax."

Climax

In this column we jot down the events that form the climax of the drama, that represent the hero's and/or heroine's attempt to straighten out the conflict that has upset their normal world. For this particular example we might write the following in the "Climax" column:

1. While driving to the banquet Alex realizes he must go tell Ellen how he feels, so he drives off to the train's destination—Lancaster, Ohio, 300 miles away.
2. Alex meets Ellen at the train station and tells her that he loves her. She tells him that she loves him too.
3. She decides not to marry old boyfriend; they kiss.

These events tell us how the conflict was resolved and should lead us to the last column, "Resolution."

Resolution

In this column we write down any shifts that we have noted in the normal state of affairs that we put down in the "Normal" column. For this example we might note, "Alex and Ellen return home as a 'couple,' but still disagree about a lot of issues—could be trouble."

We have now completed the first step of the Media Probe: we have mapped out the action of the program. Now we need to apply Media Probe Premise 2: All television examines behaviors in relationships. We address this premise by creating a "relationship string."

Relationship String

A relationship string defines the particular relationships that are of most interest to us in the program being examined. We need to do this because every program has lots of relationships in it, and it gets very difficult to follow them all. You create a relationship string by simply "stringing" the names of the characters in the relationship together at the top of a new page, for example, *Alex:Ellen*. But that is not the only relationship we could examine in this program. There are some very interesting bits of action between Alex and his mother, so we could have a sheet with the heading *Alex:Mother*. Or we could look at the ways in which Alex's relationship with his mother affected the way he behaved toward Ellen and create the following relationship string— *Mother:Alex:Ellen*.

As you can see, the possibilities are limited only by the relationships in the program. The idea is to define which relationships you and your children are most interested in examining.

Now in order to examine these relationships we need to apply the two remaining Media Probe Premises: (3) As viewers we assign motives to the behaviors that people on television display; and (4) the motives we assign to behaviors on television are based on values.

We apply these by jotting down—under the relationship string—the specific behavior we are referring to, the motive we assign to it, and the value we believe motivated the behavior. It's not as difficult as it sounds; look at the figure below.

Mother:Alex:Ellen

1. Alex is bothered by his feelings for Ellen but tells his mother he can't talk to her about it. She says OK, and leaves him alone.

Mother's Motivation: She trusts him to talk to her when he feels he is ready to.

Mother's Values:	Love	Score ____ Agree ____
	Family	Score ____ Agree ____
	Honesty	Score ____ Agree ____

Alex's Motivation: He is embarrassed to talk to his Mom about "girl problems."

| Alex's Values: | Pride | Score ____ Agree ____ |
| | Independence | Score ____ Agree ____ |

2. After talking with his mother, Alex goes after Ellen who then confides that she loves him too.

Alex's Motivation: His mother has convinced him to put pride aside in pursuit of love.

Alex's Values:	Love	Score ____ Agree ____
	Excitement	Score ____ Agree ____
	Honesty	Score ____ Agree ____

Ellen's Motivation: She left because Alex would not admit he loved her, and she was afraid to be alone. But she realized she could not get married for security without love.

Ellen's Values:	Love	Score ____ Agree ____
	Honesty	Score ____ Agree ____
	Happiness	Score ____ Agree ____

The value labels were drawn from a list that I have put together over the last dozen years, reviewing the literature, surveying my classes in media criticism, and getting input from parents in my viewing workshops. The list is not intended to be all-inclusive, but it does represent many of the values that are dealt with on television—at least many of the values that we, as parents and family members, feel are being discussed on television. Here is the list:

Accomplishment
Beauty
Excitement
Family
Freedom
Happiness
Health
Honesty
Independence
Kindness
Knowledge
Love
Money
Optimism
Power
Pride
Religion
Responsibility
Sex
Understanding
Wisdom
Work

The "Score" and "Agree" blanks let us indicate how we think the values we feel motivate the characters are treated by the program itself, *and* to what extent we agree that the program's representation of the value reflects the real world.

"Score" Blank

In this blank we indicate the extent to which we agree with the following statement. "In this story, people whose behavior reflects this value usually 'win.'" By "win" I mean come out ahead, or generally benefit from behavior based on this value. I usually ask people to restrict themselves to a simple " + , o, − " system, where " + " means agree, "o" means sometimes yes, sometimes no; and " − " means disagree. There is a tendency to want to use " + + " and " − − ," for emphasis, which is OK too.

Let us look at the first set of values on our *"Mother:Alex:Ellen"* relationship string. "Love" is the first value listed. We would score it by deciding whether people whose behavior is motivated by love come out ahead in "Family Ties." Since most of the time they do, we put " + " in that blank. Then we do the same thing with the other two until we have done each value for each situation, like this:

Mother:Alex:Ellen			
1. Alex is bothered by his feelings for Ellen but tells his mother he can't talk to her about it. She says OK, and leaves him alone.			
Mother's Motivation:	She trusts him to talk to her when he feels he is ready to.		
Mother's Values:	Love	Score +	Agree _____
	Family	Score + +	Agree _____
	Honesty	Score +	Agree _____

"Agree" Blank

In this space we indicate, using the same " + , o, − " system, the extent to which we agree with the following statement: "I believe that *in the real world*, people whose behavior is motivated by this value usually 'win,'" using the same notion of "win" that we employed in the "score" blank. If we agree that people whose motivation for behavior is love usually come out ahead we would put " + " in the "agree" blank, and we would continue through each value as we did with the "score" blanks until we came up with something like this:

Mother:Alex:Ellen			
1. Alex is bothered by his feelings for Ellen but tells his mother he can't talk to her about it. She says OK, and leaves him alone.			
Mother's Motivation:	She trusts him to talk to her when he feels he is ready to.		
Mother's Values:	Love	Score +	Agree +
	Family	Score + +	Agree +
	Honesty	Score +	Agree +

What that tells us is that we are in fairly close agreement with the values that have been represented in this particular portion of the program. But what if your fourteen-year-old daughter, who has just broken up with her boyfriend, comes up with a value score care that looks more like this:

Mother:Alex:Ellen

1. Alex is bothered by his feelings for Ellen but tells his mother he can't talk to her about it. She says OK, and leaves him alone.

Mother's Motivation: She trusts him to talk to her when he feels he is ready to.

Mother's Values:	Love	Score +	Agree -
	Family	Score + +	Agree +
	Honesty	Score +	Agree o

That score tells you that you need to have a heart-to-heart talk with your daughter about love and honesty, and young girls and broken hearts, and brighter tomorrows. And that really is the purpose of the Media Probe—it is a discussion starter. It lets us help our adolescent children explore the alternate approaches to the world presented by the media by providing a tool that helps us take apart the messages of the media, examine the values they are presenting, and decide what we—as a family—feel about those messages.

Index